How to AUTOCROSS

Andrew Howe

CarTech®

CarTech®

CarTech®, Inc.
39966 Grand Avenue
North Branch, MN 55056
Phone: 651-277-1200 or 800-551-4754
Fax: 651-277-1203
www.cartechbooks.com

Edit by Josh Brown
Layout by Elly Gosso

ISBN 978-1-61325-023-5
Item No. SA158P

Library of Congress Cataloging-in-Publication Data

Howe, Andrew.
  How to autocross / by Andrew Howe.
     p. cm.
  ISBN 978-1-932494-83-9
  1. Autocross. 2. Automobiles, Racing. 3. Compact cars–Performance. I. Title.

  GV1029.9.A88.H69 2008
  796.72–dc22
                                        2008032648

Printed in USA

Title Page:
Even in a car like the Viper, the slow corners are important. In a powerful car, corner exit speed is less important, but speed through the middle of a slow corner is critical in every car. The slower the corner, the longer the time it takes to negotiate it. (Photo Courtesy Bryan Heitkotter)

Back cover top left:
Kristi Brown drives her well-prepared G Stock class Mini Cooper S around the course. "Stock" is really just a class name, as Kristi has lightweight wheels and R-compound tires on her car. Her car is also likely sporting aftermarket shocks and exhaust. (Photo Courtesy Bryan Heitkotter)

Back cover top right:
As is common when things go awry, the driver seems to be struggling to keep his hands in good positions on the wheel–his left hand isn't even on the wheel at this moment. (Photo Courtesy Bryan Heitkotter)

Back cover middle left:
In addition to resetting the course after cars hit cones, workers are out there to help keep everyone safe. The red flags in their hands are there to wave at cars that need to stop for an unsafe situation on course. (Photo Courtesy Bryan Heitkotter)

Back cover middle right:
After the finish line, the driver has only one task: Slow the car as quickly as possible while maintaining control. The first part of that is being on the brakes as quickly as possible after the finish line. Autocross courses are typically designed with adequate, but not generous, finish chutes. (Photo Courtesy Bryan Heitkotter)

Back cover bottom left:
Strut systems don't have to be ridiculously expensive to be effective. The Eibach / Ground Control system is relatively inexpensive and does its job well. This system can be retrofitted to most dampers to make a fixed-spring system have an adjustable ride height.

Back cover bottom right:
When performing field repairs or adjustment, safety should be considered. Place jack stands under the car before starting to work. If working on hot parts like the engine or exhaust, use gloves. (Photo Courtesy Bryan Heitkotter)

CONTENTS

ACKNOWLEDGMENTS

Many thanks go out to the people who have made this book possible. Thanks to those who sucked me into the sport and educated me: Ed and Donna LaPlante, Tom Kotzian, Jim Daniels, and the Oregon Region crew. Thanks to Andy McKee, Steve Hui, and the West Coast B-Stock crowd for everything I learned in 2004. Thanks to Jerry Jenkins for being willing to have me as a co-driver, teaching me, and giving me the opportunity to meet Bryan Heitkotter. Thanks to Bryan Heitkotter for all of the fantastic photos. Thanks to my review crew for keeping me honest with the text.

And finally, thanks to my wife for putting up with my need for cars all these years.

PREFACE

This book is my contribution to the future of autocross. I didn't ask to write it; certain circumstances brought it to me. When this project was suggested to me, it came with a disclaimer: "Don't do this for the money." Like everything else in autocross, this certainly doesn't pay as well as my day job.

For several years, I have toyed with writing down all that I have learned about autocross. In the early days, it could be scribbled on the back of a note card. Now, it can be a book. By no means am I the most knowledgeable person regarding the sport of autocross. I'm far from it. But, for a book of this nature, depth of knowledge isn't necessarily the most important quality in an author. Actually, this could be much more compelling in many ways if I knew less about the sport. Now I feel obliged to dredge up some of the gory details and exceptions to the rule. I guess that's how it goes when it's time for a "memory dump"—you get the good, the bad, and the ugly.

I hope that sharing what I know will allow more people to get into the sport with a positive attitude and hang around for a while. Without a constant influx of new blood, how am I going to be able to retire to a cushy work assignment?

AUTHOR BIO

Andy Howe has been involved in autocross since 2000. He is a member of the Oregon Region of the Sports Car Club of America and has attended autocross events up and down the West Coast. In addition to driving, Andy has instructed at Novice Schools and been active in organization of autocross events. Andy has had some success at SCCA National events, including a top-five finish at the SCCA Solo National Championships. Andy lives in Salem, Oregon, with his wife, Heather, and his daughter, Katherine.

INTRODUCTION

The recent proliferation of sports cars and sport sedans has caused a boom in attendance at autocross events around the United States and Canada. This boom has brought a lot of new enthusiasm to the sport as well as some growing pains. For every novice at an autocross event who has a blast and gets hooked, there are two or three who didn't find what they were looking for. This is largely because autocross is relatively unknown to a vast majority of society. People arrive at an event with misconceptions of the sport and expectations that won't be met.

For those who survive their first few events with enthusiasm, the next hurdles can seem insurmountable. The vast gulf between the first-year autocrosser and the veteran makes it seem impossible for the beginner to compete. The sensation is overwhelming and many are discouraged. Those who choose to persevere and succeed in the sport slowly learn that progress comes in baby steps. Event by event, year by year, these drivers improve until they are the veterans.

Unfortunately, regardless of the efforts of the helpful veterans, the perception of "haves" and "have-nots" is real. While the perception is differences in car preparation or talent, the reality is differences in knowledge and experience. It's difficult for novices to check their ego at the front gate, but without any help, this is the only way a true perspective of the situation can be gained.

There have been precious few books written about autocross over the years. Among those books, only one or two have been regarded as seriously helpful to steepening the learning curve. Like those books, this book doesn't have any secrets that can't be found by attending events and asking the right people. This book should be used with other means of learning, such as driving and experimentation, to help solidify the concepts in your mind.

This book should help the novice understand the basis for the sport and give perspective to what is seen at an event. It should also offer the beginning autocrosser some ideas of what to do to improve, both in the driver's seat and in the garage, to go faster. Autocross, like other forms of racing, favors those with fatter wallets. Using this book as a reference, along with the advice of other drivers, should allow budget-minded autocrossers to pick places to get the most improvement for their dollar. For the veteran, this should be a good reference to refresh the basic concepts and to aid the novice that is struggling.

Most importantly, this book is not a how to book that can be used in a vacuum. Every situation is different. Every car and every driver are a little bit different. As such, there are no hard and fast answers. A setup that works perfectly for one driver may be unsuitable for another. This book is a reference to guide the learning process and help beginning autocrossers keep a positive attitude about the sport. Like most technical books of any value, this book should be flagged, written in, and corrected based on things learned in the course of an autocross career.

What participants take from the sport of autocross is dependent upon what they put into it. By having appropriate expectations and an understanding of how the sport can be enjoyed, a participant is more likely to have fun. Having fun entices the participant to bring more to the sport. It's a fantastic cycle and this book is a tool to start the cycle and help keep it flowing.

THE BASICS

A novice competitor in a Chevy Caprice Classic proves that you can have fun in any car. First-timers shouldn't worry about image; only having fun and learning. (Photo Courtesy Bryan Heitkotter)

An experienced competitor driving a Mazda Miata gets in over his head. The cone wedged under the front of the car is proof that he's incurred a penalty. Autocross scores are a combination of elapsed time and penalties for course deviations. (Photo Courtesy Bryan Heitkotter)

In the most fundamental sense, autocross is a test of driver skill. The skills being tested are precision and speed. Scoring is based on elapsed time required to complete a defined course and penalties applied for errors made while completing the course.

Autocross events are held all across the United States and Canada. Generally speaking, these events are designed to allow the average person to participate in his or her normal street car. Speeds do not normally exceed legal highway speeds and courses emphasize a driver's ability to maneuver an automobile in and out a series of corners. The required

safety equipment often consists of a car's factory-installed seatbelt and a helmet. If all of this sounds like it's designed for the average person, there's a reason. It is!

Autocross (sometimes called Solo racing) is the most accessible form of motorsport for the sports car enthusiast. With many clubs sanctioning events, it is possible to attend an event nearly every weekend in many areas. The low-risk format allows

drivers to participate without needing to extensively modify their car for safety. In fact, with many clubs having loaner helmets available to drivers, it is possible to simply show up to an event and compete.

Finally, because of the nature of the sport—solo competition—it is possible for drivers of many different skill levels and goals to participate together. Casual drivers out for a good time and serious competitors with deep pockets and loads of talent can attend the same event and all have fun. Autocross is what the *competitor* makes of it.

Overview of an Event

You've found a local club and want to actually try autocross. Don't be nervous and don't worry about what to expect. As a general rule (there are exceptions!), autocrossers are friendly and helpful. Ask questions if you feel the need. Most people there will be interested in helping you have a good time.

Before the Event
The work begins before you even show up. It is important to bring the appropriate things and prepare the car in an appropriate way. A few basic steps can make a huge difference between having a fun day and having a bad day.

Be prepared for a full day out. Some clubs run events where you are only obligated for half the day, but a good deal of interested novices will want to watch some of the event either before or after they compete. This means packing food and water as well as proper clothing for the season. If the forecast includes a chance

of rain, pack a full change of clothes. Be prepared to put all of your possessions out in the elements while you are driving. It is common to see watertight totes or tarps at autocrosses. If the forecast is for sun, pack sunscreen and lots of water. Be sure to have proper shoes for driving—sandals aren't typically allowed. Also, be sure to pack shoes for walking and running, as both of these activities are common at an autocross.

Preparing the car is pretty simple if it is well maintained. A recent oil change isn't a bad idea, but making sure that the oil level is sufficient should be the minimum. Take everything out of the car that you don't need at the event. Loose items are not permitted in the car. Imagine driving around with a bowling ball in the trunk! This is where you consider how valuable an item is and how comfortable you would feel leaving it unattended for two hours. Valuables and other precious items should be left at home.

Another key step to preparing for an autocross is to inflate the tires, especially the front tires, to near their maximum recommended pressure as indicated on the sidewall. High-performance driving stresses tires differently than a casual trip to the

supermarket, and normal street tires are not going to be happy at 30 psi.

The last key of preparation for the event is to plan on arriving early. There is a lot to do before the driver's meeting and time sneaks away. Having the time to relax and ask questions is important to having fun. Otherwise, the event may feel like work as you are rushed around the whole time. If nothing else, you'll have extra time to walk the course.

The Liability Waiver
Upon arriving at the event site, the very first thing to do is carefully read and sign the liability waiver. This form is to release everyone on site from liability. Generally speaking, it says that anyone signing the waiver understands that there is some risk associated with the event and that these risks include property damage, physical injury, and death. A good waiver will state that everyone signing the form understands the risks, has inspected the site, and waives the right to pursue compensation from others signing the waiver due to what may happen at the event. A responsible participant

The driver of a Subaru Impreza WRX STi drags a cone away from the scene of the crime. While loss of control and accidents do happen occasionally at autocross events, scuffing a bumper while crushing a cone is the most typical incident. A good coat of wax before an event can even help the cone mark buff right out. (Photo Courtesy Bryan Heitkotter)

The paddock at an event is typically cluttered with autocross paraphernalia. The unattended yard sale look is common, but events are reasonably secure. Still, safeguard your valuables. (Photo Courtesy Bryan Heitkotter)

A Mazda Miata driver tempts the wrath of the convertible gods by running with the top up. Autocross events happen in rain or shine. Pack accordingly. (Photo Courtesy Bryan Heitkotter)

will read the waiver and continuously watch for unsafe situations during the event.

Accidents can happen. It is important that all participants understand the potential risks of attending an event and how to minimize those risks. The easiest way to limit the risks for all participants and organizers is for everyone on the event site to read and sign the liability waiver. In most clubs, signing the waiver is a requirement to attend the event—whether you choose to participate or not.

Registration

Registration procedures and fees vary from club to club. Most clubs are happy to have people who are not club members participate in their events, but some clubs do require membership to participate. Expect to pay more than $20 for the privilege to participate. Make sure you have a valid driver's license—this is required to participate in nearly all autocross events.

Technical Inspection

Technical inspection is required at all autocross events. The purpose of this inspection is to ensure that all cars that will be driven meet at least a minimum level of safety. It is common for the inspection to include checking of seat belts, lug nuts, wheel bearings, brakes, and throttle, and making sure there are no loose items in or on the car. Nearly all new cars pass a technical inspection, though the inspector may require the removal of hubcaps, floor mats, and other loose items.

Tall vehicles, such as trucks, sport utility vehicles, and vans, are not likely to be allowed on course simply because of their high centers of gravity. These vehicles are more likely to roll over during aggressive

driving and many clubs have prohibited their use for the safety of all participants—drivers and course workers alike.

It is also common for the inspection to include making sure that the helmet to be used meets the required standard. For Sports Car Club of America (SCCA) events, the standard is Snell M or SA rating that is either the most current standard or one of the two previous standards. For example, if the current standard were Snell 2005, the previous two standards would be Snell 2000 and Snell 95. Any helmet rated either M or SA bearing these standard designations would be acceptable. Snell rating stickers are typically found inside the helmet's lining. If you don't own a helmet, be sure to ask the person doing the inspections about the acceptable standards before you buy one.

Work Assignment

Every participant in an autocross event is expected to work to help make the event run smoothly. Autocross is so affordable and accessible because it does not require hiring workers or finding large numbers of volunteers. The catch is that this

A worker aligns the timing lights at an event. This is just one job that has to get done before an event can begin. Note the checkered wristband on the worker. This indicates that he has signed the insurance waiver for the event. (Photo Courtesy Bryan Heitkotter)

means the drivers need to work to make the event happen. It is important to both sign up for a work assignment and work at the assigned place and time. Failure to work will generally start you off on the wrong foot with a club and may get you disqualified from the event. If you have a question about the work assignment, be sure to ask the person making the assignments.

Some clubs don't require first-time autocrossers to work. It is the opinion of some clubs that it is more important for first-timers to watch and see how the event operates rather than making them work at their very first event. These clubs are great for novices!

A course worker raises a cone to indicate a penalty. Course workers are the most important part of an event because they watch everything that happens on course. A mistake by a course worker can mean the difference between a good day and a bad day for an autocrosser.

Cones and chalk lines mark the course. The cones lying down are called "pointer" cones and are there for directional purposes only. The cones standing up mark the course. The chalk lines are put down for direction only and can be driven over without penalty. (Photo Courtesy Bryan Heitkotter)

Grid is where the on-course action starts. It's usually packed with cars and people. It's a great place to find help between runs, but don't get too far from your car. You wouldn't want to miss a run!

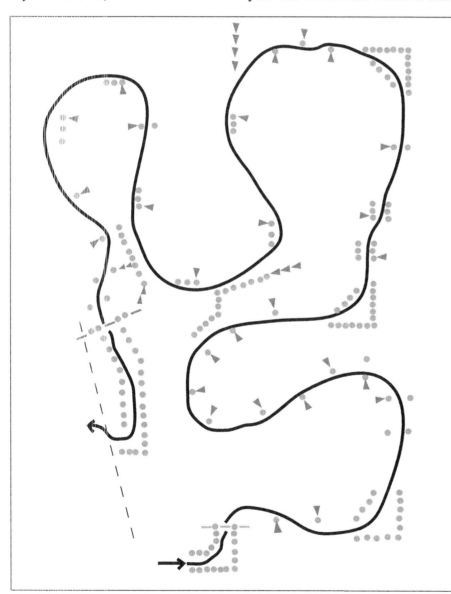

Competitors are out walking the course before an event. Each competitor needs to walk the course before getting in the car to drive. It's not necessary to memorize the course, but you do need an idea of where you are going. (Photo Courtesy Bryan Heitkotter)

Most autocross events have a course map available at registration. Pick one up and take it with you. When walking the course, remember that the course map is for information only and is probably not drawn to scale. Make your plans based on what you see on the pavement.

Here's an example of bringing almost everything to grid. They've got tire blankets, a water sprayer, an air compressor, helmets, a floor jack, and probably some stuff still in the car. The kitchen sink is in there somewhere. With grid so crowded, think about whether you really need something before you bring it.

In addition to resetting the course after cars hit cones, workers are out there to help keep everyone safe. The red flags in their hands are there to wave at cars that need to stop for an unsafe situation on course. (Photo Courtesy Bryan Heitkotter)

Walking the Course

Many events have a map of the course available at registration. While this is helpful for knowing in general what the course looks like, *walking the course is crucial*. Autocross doesn't typically have practice runs, so walking the course is the only way to see the course before competition. Again...*walking the course is crucial!*

It is common for novice first-time autocrossers to be overwhelmed by the whole scene. It looks like a sea of cones! If possible, find an experienced driver to walk with and have him or her help you read the scene. Many clubs will have experienced drivers who have, as their work assignment, the job of finding novice drivers and helping them find their way around the course. Try to walk the course until you have a good idea of its layout.

The Grid

The grid is a special part of the event site. Cars that are competing or are about to compete are parked in the grid. The grid is often crowded and busy. Keep on your toes at all times. It's easy to step backward in front of a moving car.

Move your car into the appropriate grid at the appropriate time. If you have questions about where you should be, ask someone. Workers will direct you from the grid to the starting line at the appropriate time. An almost-universal rule at autocross events is that once the grid is set, it doesn't change. This means that you almost always follow the car in front of you. If the grid needs to change, someone will tell you.

Also, try not to bring any unnecessary items into the grid—they may get inadvertently damaged while

A driver at a regional event is participating just for the fun of it. Many clubs have "Fun Run" classes for drivers who want to enjoy the sport without worrying about classes. This is a great way to enjoy the sport and learn. (Photo Courtesy Bryan Heitkotter)

Course workers hustle to reset cones between cars. Events often happen at a fast pace. In addition to driving fast, workers need to be alert to get the course reset before the next driver. (Photo Courtesy Bryan Heitkotter)

Passengers

Many clubs allow passengers to ride along during autocross runs. This is a great way for a non-competitor to get a feel for the sport. A prospective autocrosser might want to ride along with an experienced driver to get an idea of what the sport is like. It's a great way to break the ice and introduce new people to the sport.

Most clubs that allow passengers also have restrictions on passengers for novice competitors. These clubs don't allow first-timers to take their friends out on course. The idea here is safety. The club doesn't want to take any unnecessary risks, and novice drivers don't need any additional distractions in the car. This doesn't mean that novices can't have passengers at all.

It is common for clubs to allow novices to take an instructor out on course. The purpose here is to help the novice be more comfortable and learn faster. Instruction can be as simple as helping the driver find the course or as important as calming down a driver with too much enthusiasm. Regardless of the reason, if you want instruction, ask for it! If an instructor asks to ride with you and help you out, take him or her up on the offer. Novices who receive one-on-one help generally learn faster and enjoy the event more than those who don't.

Also, if the club allows it, ask to ride along with another driver. Seeing how they drive will make the transition from the street to the autocross course easier. Don't be upset if they tell you no (they might be in tight competition and

cars and people move about in a bit of a hurry. Others will have lots of stuff—tire pressure gauges, air compressors, tire blankets, etc.—so bring the minimum to the grid. A granola bar, a bottle of water, and a helmet are good choices. At your first event, just about everything else can stay in the paddock.

Driver's Meeting

At nearly every autocross event, there is a driver's meeting. The meeting typically covers items regarding safety, appropriate conduct while at the event, some basic rules of event operations, and gives drivers a chance to ask questions. Many experienced autocrossers will rudely talk through the meeting—they've heard it all before (often quite literally).

This meeting is especially important for a first-timer. Be sure to hear what is being said and ask any questions you may have. The event organizer may ask novice competitors to hang around after the general meeting to cover a couple items of importance, such as penalties for course deviation or availability of driving instructors for help.

Working the Event

Remember that work assignment from several steps ago? It's time to do whatever the assignment is. A typical work assignment will last between 1 and 1-1/2 hours—roughly equal to the amount of time required to run one heat of competition. Be early, be helpful, and be attentive. The range of work assignments runs from working the insurance waiver table, to crowd control, to working on the course (running and resetting cones, calling penalties), to working in the grid, to working in timing and scoring. However insignificant the job may seem, it is important to the successful running of the event. The better you do your job, the more likely it is that others will be having fun.

Sometimes the work assignment is performed before driving; sometimes it is done after driving. Be sure to know when you are assigned to work. It is easy to get confused with so much going on. If in doubt, ask.

Some drivers are very serious about the sport. Multi-time SCCA National Champion Andy McKee has prepared his Mazda RX-7 to the limits of his class (SM2) rules and well beyond what is legal (or practical) on the street. (Photo Courtesy Bryan Heitkotter)

Driving!

After all of that, you can drive. Relax and have fun. A first-time autocrosser should have only two goals: successfully and safely complete the course without penalty and have fun! If a first-timer achieves this goal and still has more runs, the only goal is improving the time and car-control skills. Although it is tempting, there should be no serious thoughts of being competitive with veteran drivers, as it is easy to be discouraged by making comparisons.

Many first-time autocrossers are disappointed that they spend half a day at an event and only get a few minutes of driving time. This is nor-

Many clubs use large reader boards like this one to display a driver's time. This is for information only, as official times are read off a different device and recorded onto the run cards. (Photo Courtesy Bryan Heitkotter)

Vic Sias demonstrates one way to drive while carrying an autocross timeslip. Lots of clubs have a worker placed after the finish line to write down the unofficial time for you. This means you don't have to worry about trying to see the reader board while slowing down. (Photo Courtesy Bryan Heitkotter)

mal. At a typical event, a driver can expect to get three to five runs that last between 30 and 60 seconds each. Autocross isn't about getting a lot of seat time—it is about the quality of that seat time. A typical autocross course has more corners than a road race circuit and drivers will finish the course in less time than it takes to complete one lap on most circuits.

Some first-timers don't return for a second event because they didn't feel the amount of driving time was enough. For most experienced drivers, an autocross event is as much social as it is competitive. To get the most out of the sport, beginners should go out of their way to start making friends and finding people to help them along. A good way to do this is to find other people with similar cars and ask them about their cars and car preparation. Think of it as spending half a day with friends and getting to drive rather than spending half a day to drive a few minutes.

Scoring an Event

Autocross events are scored based on two components. The first component is the elapsed time between the starting lights and the

A competitor is adding air to the tires in the paddock. The portable air compressor and tire pressure gauge are great tools for the autocrosser. This driver also has wooden blocks under the tire to get the car high enough for his floor jack.

finish lights. The second component is penalties that are assessed for course deviations. Penalties can vary from club to club, but the generally accepted standard is a two-second penalty for each cone that is displaced (all standing cones typically count). The other deviation from the defined course is called missing a gate, or a "gate penalty." Rules vary widely on gate penalties and it's not uncommon to be scored "Did Not Finish" (DNF) on runs where a gate is missed. In most competitive classes, a run with any penalty will not win an event. So, the emphasis should be on clean, fast runs.

Basic Autocross Gear

Most autocrossers have a list of essential items that they carry to every event. This list varies greatly from driver to driver and car to car. The following list covers the basic autocross accessories that many folks bring with them to every event.

Portable Air Compressor

Autocrossers carry portable air compressors with them so that they can add air to their tires at the event. Some clubs have compressors available for use, but not all do. Even if there is a compressor available for general use, it may be difficult to access it between runs.

Compressors come in two general varieties: powered by rechargeable batteries and powered off of a car's cigarette lighter outlet. Obviously each type has its own advantage, but the most popular units seem to be battery powered. Regardless of type, durability is very important. The compressor will likely be tossed around somewhat during the autocross season.

Portable Air Tank

The air tank serves the same purpose as the air compressor. The tank needs to be filled at a compressor, but after it is filled it doesn't need any power. The tank is much quieter than a portable compressor but has a limited supply of compressed air for filling tires. With the availability of high-quality, inexpensive portable air compressors, the portable air tank is less common than it once was.

Tire Pressure Gauge

A good tire pressure gauge is important. The tires are the only part of the car that is touching the pavement and are what starts, stops, and turns the car. A high-quality gauge is necessary to make sure that the tires are properly inflated. The most popular gauges have large dials and bleed valves that can be used to release air from the tire without needing to disconnect the gauge.

Tire Blankets

Most high-performance tires should be warm for optimum performance. Recent advances in tire technology have lowered the optimum temperature for high-performance tires, but these tires operate at temperatures above 100 degrees F. At the start of the event, the tires are ambient temperature—likely not warm enough to perform at their best. After completing the first run of an event, the tires will have some heat in them. Serious competitors place tire blankets on the tires to retain this heat if they think the tires will cool off too much before their next run on the course.

Water Sprayer

Water sprayers are becoming more common in the grid. With the lowering of the optimum operating temperature for high-performance tires, drivers are finding the need to cool their tires back down to the correct temperature before their next run. The sprayers are used to apply water to the rubber of the tires and, thus, evaporation cools everything down.

Additionally, water sprayers are often used to cool key engine components between runs. It is common to see intake manifolds, intercoolers, and radiators being cooled between runs to prevent an engine from "heat soaking." Serious competitors use any legal means to gain a performance advantage and, generally speaking, cooling components between runs is legal.

A driver in a Mistubishi Evolution gets some help in grid. A second set of hands in grid isn't necessary, but it can be helpful. If time between runs is short, having someone help you cool your tires can relieve some stress. (Photo Courtesy Bryan Heitkotter)

How do you haul tires when you're driving a Corvette? A tire trailer, of course! This autocrosser has two sets of tires on his trailer—one set for dry track and one set for wet.

Removable Numbers & Letters

Magnetic and static-cling numbers and letters are commonly used to display a car's classification and car number. Each club has a desired size for the car number and class designation for competitors. The use of removable numbers and letters allow competitors to quickly apply and remove the appropriate information. This allows the driver to properly display needed information at the event without drawing unwanted attention away from the event.

The SCCA's rulebook specifies a minimum size for class numbers and letters. Car numbers are supposed to be 8 inches tall and class letters are supposed to be 4 inches tall. Not all clubs enforce these rules, but if you were going to invest in removable numbers, it would be good to meet these minimums.

First-timers: Don't fret if you don't have magnetic or static-cling numbers, however. Other solutions include blue painter's tape or a sheet of paper with large numbers hand printed on it and taped to the inside of a window. Be warned, however: While some clubs allow white shoe

The Street Touring classes are relatively new but very popular. The concept of this category is to allow lightly modified common sedans and low-powered sports cars a place to compete on street tires. The requirement to run a true street tire means that these cars are often driven straight off the street and onto the course. (Photo Courtesy Bryan Heitkotter)

polish, it's generally a bad plan. In addition to being difficult to remove if it gets onto the black rubber around the window, shoe polish will run if it rains.

Tire Trailers

Tire trailers are small utility trailers that can easily be towed behind a sports car. A trailer hitch is a prerequisite for using a tire trailer to tow race tires. Sports cars aren't commonly equipped with these from the factory, but several companies manufacture hitches for sports cars. If you've wondered how to pack a set of four race tires to an event when you're driving a Miata, this is how it's done.

Miscellaneous

The list of miscellaneous varies from driver to driver and car to car. Floor jacks, portable impact guns, and torque wrenches are all common for people who change tires at autocross events. Another group of folks tow their racecars on a trailer. Some people carry half a car's worth of spare parts and a service manual, and some folks don't carry more than an extra quart of oil.

Classes: How to Decide Which is for You

True beginners should care little about what class their car falls into.

Stock class cars can be straight off the street, like this Acura RSX. In Stock, the emphasis is on driver skill rather than car preparation, and drivers can be competitive with minimal modifications to the car. (Photo Courtesy Bryan Heitkotter)

C Street Prepared is one of the most popular classes in autocross. The mainstay of this class is the moderately modified Mazda Miata. With these cars being both inexpensive and fun to drive, it's easy to see why CSP is a hit. (Photo Courtesy Bryan Heitkotter)

But, as drivers become more involved with the sport, car classing becomes a concern. Few competitors are content with no realistic chance to ever win. For clubs using the SCCA's classing system, the classes can be found in the SCCA Solo Rulebook (available online for free or hard copy for a price.) For other systems, make sure to ask the event organizers for a set of rules.

It is common for new drivers to start autocrossing in whatever they have. Unfortunately, their car is often either ill suited to autocross or has been modified for the fun of driving rather than prepared to a particular rule set. When drivers become more comfortable with their club and the flow of an event, they realize that their car is completely noncompetitive. It is also easy to be frustrated by a rulebook that is difficult to understand. This commonly leads to two types of questions: Why is my car in Class X? Why does modification Q bump me into Class Y?

At this point, an autocrosser has to answer this question: Am I here just to have fun or am I here to compete, too?

If a driver is just out to have fun, car classification should be completely irrelevant. Most clubs allow "Time Only" entries for just this case. This type of driver should find someone else in the club in a similar car and compare times to measure improvement over time.

Those who want to compete should decide how dedicated they are to their new hobby. It must be understood that, for competitors, the class rules come first and the car preparation is secondary.

The casual competitor should pick a class that looks like fun and prepare the car to that set of rules. It may not sound like fun, but choosing a class and set of rules first makes competing much more enjoyable. This can mean deciding not to make a particular modification or even removing a

modification from the car. It may also mean adding a modification that wasn't previously considered.

More serious competitors make larger sacrifices for the sport. It is common for newer autocrossers to buy a new autocross car (or at least new to them!) after a season or two. The purchase of a new vehicle allows a driver to select both a class and a car, enhancing the chances of success and, hopefully, have more fun. After buying a new car, the car is prepared according to the rules of the class by choosing the legal modifications with the most performance benefit on an autocross course. Hopefully, the driver has a budget and can stick to it. It is not necessary to use every allowance in the rulebook in order to be competitive and have fun.

The most serious autocrossers are not often novices. Clubs often have a few veteran drivers who have purchased "the car" for a particular class and prepared it to the limit of the

C Prepared is a special group of competitors. These cars are highly modified American muscle. Prepared class cars seldom see the street, but they're awesome to watch. (Photo Courtesy Bryan Heitkotter)

Formula 125 is a new and popular class for karts. This class allows 125-cc shifter carts to compete on an autocross course. Not all sites are suitable for karts, so it's best to do some homework before bringing a kart to an event. (Photo Courtesy

rules. These drivers are often very fast—sometimes seconds faster than anyone else in the class—and the temptation is there to try to compete with them. Novices should not travel down this path without significant guidance from a veteran. At the highest level of preparation, even in the classes with the fewest preparation allowances, it is easy to spend vast sums of money and make little real progress. This is the fastest way to sour someone on the sport.

A final word on classes and car preparation: Choose a class and car (and car preparation) that you can afford—in both time and money. A heavily modified class may look like a lot of fun, but understand that less restrictive rules mean spending more money and working harder to prepare the car in order to be competitive. Choose the right class for the right reasons.

Why is "Stock" Not Stock? Do I Need Race Tires?

With a name like "Stock Category," one might think the SCCA's family of Stock classes is a place that a car straight off the street can be competitive. Don't let the name fool you. Stock is a level of preparation, not a description of the cars. The list of allowed modifications in this category is small, but that hasn't stopped serious competitors from taking advantage of every allowance in the rulebook in the quest for a National Championship. The same can be said of the rest of the SCCA categories.

The classes published in the SCCA Solo rulebook are intended for national level competition. These classes don't necessarily meet an individual's wants or needs. If your local club is using the SCCA rulebook as the skeleton of their classing system, check out their supplemental classes before jumping into the appropriate SCCA class. If the SCCA rule set doesn't work well for you, you're not alone. Many clubs, including SCCA regional clubs, have added their own classes that suit their members better than the SCCA National classes.

Commonly added classes are "Open Street" and "Street Tire." The Open Street class generally allows almost any car that is (or was) street legal. This class is what spawned "Street Modified" in the SCCA rulebook, but Open Street is generally less restrictive in every way. The Street Tire class generally allows cars that would have fallen into Stock, Street Prepared, and Street Modified classes to compete on true street tires (rather than United States Department of Transportation/DOT-legal autocross "slicks"). These classes are commonly indexed with a system referred to as the "PAX" or "RTP." This indexing system allows times from different classes to be compared, somewhat like bracket racing. The PAX/RTP index system is explained in depth in Chapter 10.

Kristi Brown drives her well-prepared G Stock class Mini Cooper S around the course. "Stock" is really just a class name, as Kristi has lightweight wheels and R-compound tires on her car. Her car is also likely sporting aftermarket shocks and exhaust. (Photo Courtesy Bryan Heitkotter)

The alphabet soup on the door of this car indicates a driver that has found a class specifically for them. This driver is driving a C Street Prepared class car in an indexed street tire class specifically for ladies. Not every club has a class like this, but odds are you can find a class that suits you well. (Photo Courtesy Bryan Heitkotter)

CAR CONTROL

You know how to drive a car. If you didn't, you wouldn't be interested in autocross and you wouldn't have bought this book. Autocross requires that a driver's skills be tested on another level. Autocross explores the absolute limits of a driver's talent. Mostly, autocross shows us our shortcomings. This chapter points out common flaws in driving technique that are often of little consequence on the highway, but can be very detrimental on the autocross course.

It can be very difficult to identify problems in driving technique by ourselves. The driver is often too busy driving the car to see either the good or the bad. A driver who has access to instruction and attempts to apply these rules all the time (on the highway and the autocross course) will generally quickly cure themselves of bad habits. These skills must be learned by doing them. The key to mastery is repetition.

Seating Position: Hands and Feet

It might not seem related to car control, but seating position has a lot to do with what a driver can and can't do. Seating position determines where the hands and feet are and how they can be used. Seating position is the foundation for proper technique. With an improper seat position, you could be at a disadvantage before you even move from the starting line!

Let's start with the seat base. The position of the seat base is determined by how long a driver's legs are. A driver should be able to fully depress all of the pedals without completely straightening his or her legs. Alternatively, the legs should be straight enough that the knees don't interfere with turning the steering wheel. This leaves us with the idea that the knees should be slightly bent with the pedal fully depressed. This position allows the driver to use the strength of their legs if needed but still allow the driver to use the ankle to make fine adjustments like modulating the brake pedal. A car's pedals aren't switches, and proper seating position allows the driver to make small adjustment when needed.

The upper body should be placed so that the hands rest at roughly 9 o'clock and 3 o'clock on the steering wheel and the elbows bent at

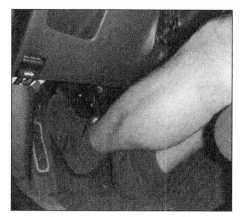

This seating position is acceptable for the legs. The left leg is not fully straightened even though the clutch is fully depressed. The right leg is in a similar position. Note that the ankles, specifically, are not fully extended. This allows the driver the ability to modulate the pedal pressure with the ankle, affording greater control over the car.

approximately 90-degree angles. One technique that has been used to set upper body position is to reach the arms straight out and place the wrists on the top of the steering wheel. Adjust the seat back so that one of these cases is true.

With luck, you can still see the road and your head isn't crammed into the roof of the car. At this point,

Aftermarket Seat Belts

Having trouble staying in your seat? With the proliferation of leather seats and the reel-style, three-point belts that are standard on modern cars, it's easy to slide around. For those who left-foot brake and can't use their left foot to push themselves back into the seat, this is a serious problem. Autocrossers commonly add driver restraints to their cars to help hold them in their seat. These devices come in several varieties, each with its own advantages and disadvantages.

Aftermarket lap belts have been around for many years. They are very similar to the seat belts of old—a single belt that is hard to adjust. These are typically mounted to the standard lower mounting points for the factory seat belt system and, when not in use,

The Schroth harness is the only street-legal four- or five-point harness on the market today. It is a good fit for cars with race seats and does a superb job holding the driver in the seat. The combination of a race seat and a four-point harness means the driver never needs to worry about sliding around.

stow easily behind or under the seat. The disadvantage of this system is that it does nothing to restrain the upper body.

Aftermarket three- and four-point harnesses that are legal for street use have become increasingly common. These belts typically separate the shoulder harness adjustment from the lap belt adjustment, allowing the driver to really secure themselves into their seat. These harnesses often prevent the seat behind the driver from being used when the harness is in use. Another drawback is that these harnesses often don't stow away very easily when not in use. The final drawback is that many clubs prohibit the use of aftermarket shoulder harnesses in convertibles without roll bars.

The CG Lock and similar devices are adapters to alter the way the factory seat belts function. The concept here is to fix the length of the lap belt without requiring the installation of aftermarket seat belts. These devices work in much the same way that the supplemental locks for child safety seats work. The driver sets the lap belt length and then locks the device onto the seat belt where the belt turns from the lap to the shoulder. The device prevents the belt from sliding through the latch, fixing the length of the lap belt.

Regardless of the method chosen, the manufacturer's recommendations need to be strictly followed. These devices do not function like the factory restraint belts, and supplemental restraint systems like airbags may not function as designed. Improper installation or use of the belt can result in serious injury in the event of an accident.

This driver is using a Schroth harness. Unfortunately, he looks rather distracted at this moment. Hitting a cone can cause a driver to lose focus as it usually means that the run is lost. Continuing along fully focused can help a driver learn something about the course that is useful for subsequent runs. (Photo Courtesy Bryan Heitkotter)

The driver of this Miata has used a common trick among autocrossers. The rear view mirror is turned so that it doesn't obstruct the driver's vision any more than necessary. An autocrosser shouldn't ever be looking in the mirror while on course, and the extra visibility doesn't hurt. (Photo Courtesy Bryan Heitkotter)

Here, the upper body is shown. The driver's elbows are bent at nearly 90 degrees with the hands placed at 9 and 3 on the steering wheel. Note the "thumbs up" posture of the hands for easy shuffling of the steering wheel.

Driving an A Modified class car in the rain doesn't seem like much fun. This driver is showing a good seating position for control with hands at 10 and 2. The wheel is gripped firmly as shuffling the steering wheel is not a common need on formula cars. (Photo Courtesy Bryan Heitkotter)

make adjustments with the seat height and steering column location as required. Test your seating position with your helmet on to make sure your head movement isn't restricted in any way. Try your new seating position on the street to get used to it before attending an event.

Hand Position

Now that the seating position has been set, what do you do with your hands? Hands should be kept in "strong" positions. This allows the driver to maintain control of the car and be able to make fine adjustments. The most common hand positions are left hand between 9 and 10 o'clock and right hand between 2 and 3 o'clock. These positions are "thumbs up" with hands at or above the mid-height of the wheel. Hands should never rest on the shifter!

Hands should not be placed on the top or bottom of the steering wheel as a starting position. Hands at the top and bottom of the steering wheel are in very weak positions and it is difficult to maintain control of the wheel. If you want to test this out, hold your hands in these positions and have a friend gently push or pull on them. Try this again with the "thumbs up" position and the difference will be clear.

Some drivers turn their thumbs in and grip the steering wheel like a baseball bat. This gives good leverage on the wheel, but will slow down hand movement when moving hands around the steering wheel. This one really comes down to an individual driver's need and preference and, other than speed when shuffling the wheel or strength of grip in a manual steering car, there isn't a strong argument either way.

This Mazda RX-8 has been driven to a nice, tight apex. The driver should be preparing to unwind the steering wheel and apply throttle. The fastest drivers at autocross events are generally the first to apply the throttle when leaving a corner. Hopefully, the brake lights are still on because the driver is a left-foot braker. (Photo Courtesy Bryan Heitkotter)

Bad Habits

How did you get so many bad habits? Driving on the street! For most of us, our first driving instructors had no idea about performance driving. We learned from their example (commonly in an automatic) and then, over the years, adapted to what was comfortable for us. All of those "comfortable" habits happen subconsciously. So, we practice them when autocrossing as well.

To break bad habits (or start new good habits) on the autocross course, we must change our everyday driving habits. In everyday driving, we can focus more intently on our driving habits and less on where we're going—we're not flying through the cones! Also, we spend much, much, much more time driving on the street than we do on an autocross course. Even if you drive at an autocross event every weekend, odds are that you'll have significantly more seat time on the street than on the course. Since the street is where we usually drive, the street is where we start making our good habits for the autocross course.

This driver is showing good car control habits. The driver's hands are in a strong position with the right hand at 1 o'clock. The driver's eyes are looking ahead, out the driver's side window of the car. (Photo Courtesy Bryan Heitkotter)

Uh-oh. This driver has let things get a little out of hand. A very large steering correction has been made. As is common when things go awry, the driver seems to be struggling to keep his hands in good positions on the wheel—his left hand isn't even on the wheel at this moment. (Photo Courtesy Bryan Heitkotter)

Steering Inputs: Using Your Hands

Hands have two distinct jobs when autocrossing: steering and shifting. If you're not shifting, both hands should be on the wheel, steering. Lots of people drive with one hand on the wheel and one hand resting on the shift knob. Many of these people don't even know they're doing it. If this is you...stop it!

Previously we discussed where to put your hands. In practice, your hands are constantly moving as you steer the car. We want to keep your hands on the wheel as much as possible, but we also want to maintain strong hand positions. We want to do both in order to maintain the best control possible.

In road racing, it is common to hear coaching to never move the left hand on the steering wheel. This is not true of autocrossing. Autocrossers need to turn the wheel sharper than is necessary on a road course. Simply put, you MUST move your hands to maintain control.

When steering an autocross car, the steering wheel should be shuffled through the hands in order to maintain a reasonable hand position. The hands should remain in reasonably strong positions at all times—shuffle your hands before your left hand reaches 3 o'clock! Avoid crossing your hands, even when shuffling. Shuffling goes like this:

While holding wheel firmly with left hand, release grip with right hand and slide right hand toward left hand until it is in a strong position. Grip the wheel firmly with your right hand and release grip with your left hand. Slide your left hand away from your right hand until it is in a strong position. Re-grip wheel with

This Miata pilot has not shuffled his hands as he entered the corner. Note that the driver's right hand has crossed over to the left side of the steering wheel. An unrelated issue is the brake lockup. The driver is braking late and the combination of braking and cornering has caused the left front wheel to lock. (Photo Courtesy Bryan Heitkotter)

the left hand. To shuffle back, reverse the process.

Another trick to controlling the car is to have soft hands. Grip the wheel only as tightly as is required to control the steering wheel. The "death grip" is rather common, but not at all helpful. Such a grip means it will take longer to shuffle the hands. The death grip also prevents the driver from feeling the light pressure on the wheel caused by the car's feedback. This information can be important so, using soft hands is an advantage.

Finally, don't let the steering wheel slide through your hands and then grab it. Using a car's self-centering steering wheel is a lazy way of returning the wheel to center after a corner and a very common habit on the street. There are two reasons that this habit must be broken: The driver has no control of the wheel if there are no hands on it and re-grabbing the wheel will shock the car slightly.

On the street, things are happening slowly and neither of these items is typically concerning. On the autocross course, they can both cause trouble.

Looking Ahead

Let's face it, if your eyes are always focused 30 feet in front of the car, you have no idea where you're really going. The first step toward putting the car where you want it is to look farther ahead and see where you want to go. As far as car control fundamentals go, looking ahead is the most important single skill.

When driving, a driver's eyes should scan ahead down the course at all times. Under normal circumstances, little, if any, attention should be given to what is right in front of the car. You can have little effect on where the car will be in one second. On the other hand, you have a lot of control over where you will be three to five seconds down the course. That is where you need to be looking.

The first thing to be gained by looking ahead is early recognition of upcoming course elements. It is

Ron Bauer, a Solo National Champion, is entering a corner. Ron's eyes are already picking up the corner exit. He appears to be off the brakes already and preparing to accelerate out of the corner. (Photo Courtesy Bryan Heitkotter)

Now a little deeper into the corner, Ron is looking out the passenger side of the car. The wheel is turned hard and the car is at peak cornering force. Looking ahead causes the driver to naturally start unwinding the steering wheel. (Photo Courtesy Bryan Heitkotter)

As the corner exit is approached, Ron's eyes start returning to the windshield. As the eyes return to the front, the hands start unwinding the steering wheel. At the same time, the driver can start to accelerate out of the corner. (Photo Courtesy Bryan Heitkotter)

Looking ahead has advantages beyond quicker run times. A driver who looks ahead has a better chance to see other important things, such as a corner worker waving a red flag. This makes looking ahead more than just about going fast. It's about being safe. (Photo Courtesy Bryan Heitkotter)

This BMW driver is looking out the side window to see the course. When the course gets tight and slow, looking ahead typically requires looking out the side of the car. In this case, looking out the windshield would limit visibility of the course to around one second. (Photo Courtesy Bryan Heitkotter)

easier to prepare for a corner if you know it's coming. A driver who looks ahead will not need to rely completely on course memorization to know where he or she is going. Also, a driver who looks ahead will have a better chance of seeing unexpected things, such as red flags, course workers, misplaced cones, and the like.

The second important thing about looking ahead is really simple, but often forgotten. The car will go where you look. If, as you approach a corner, you look at the apex, you'll driver there. When approaching the apex, your eyes should be looking at the exit of the corner...so the car will drive there. With autocross courses being full of tight corners, a driver's eyes will sometimes be looking out the side windows of the car. This is OK. In fact, it's a good sign.

It's easy to find ourselves looking at the wrong things. When looking down the course, we often look at the inside of a corner before we get there. This causes you to slowly drift toward the inside of the curve. Discipline with the eyes is key. Always look where you want to go.

It is common to focus on or even stare at an apex cone. Focusing on the apex cone will cause you to drive to the cone, usually on an undesired line. If you find yourself falling victim to this, try to pick something to look at that keeps you on your desired line. Wait another half second before looking at the apex and then look at it briefly before moving your eyes to the exit of the corner.

The Friction Circle

The friction circle is a graphic representation of the traction available. The friction circle shows you that using traction to brake or accelerate reduces the amount of traction available for cornering. It is most conveniently applied to the motion of the entire car, but the friction circle can be applied to each individual tire, as well.

The driver of this Mazda Protégé seems pretty focused on the cone he's sliding toward. As long as his eyes stay on the cone, he will likely succeed in hitting it. If he looks down the course, away from this cone, his chances of escaping the cone penalty are much better. (Photo Courtesy Bryan Heitkotter)

Slip Angles

What is a slip angle? It is the difference between the direction the tire is rolling and the direction the tire is moving. If the slip angle of a tire is zero, the tire is not making any cornering force. If the slip angle of all the tires is zero, the car is going straight. Or you've got a very rare four-wheel steering system!

The significance of the slip angle is that it determines how much cornering force is generated. A tire can generate force in two directions—fore and aft (by accelerating or braking) and laterally (from friction generated by the slip angle). The magnitude of the lateral force is dependent upon the slip angle of the tire.

As the slip angle is increased, the cornering force is increased. At some point, increasing the slip angle begins to reduce the cornering force. This angle varies somewhat from tire to tire and surface to surface because of the molecular interactions between the tire and the pavement. For our purposes, slip angle can be taken as between 10 and 15 degrees. Slip angles greater than this, while often fun, are not fast.

A by-product of generating cornering force is the addition of drag. Drag slows the car. It isn't obvious that turning the car will result in slowing the car until the slip angle is considered. The vector addition proves it. Cornering slows the car.

In the end, this is technical talk. While it is absolutely critical to understand the slip angle for an engineer working on a racecar, a driver doesn't need to know the techno-talk. It has been included to give some background for other discussions. If this sort of thing interests you, you might want to read *Tune to Win* by Carroll Smith and other racecar engineering books.

Even when the car is clearly under control and the car is being driven as well as possible, cornering slows the car. The slip angle that generates cornering force also generates a small amount of drag. A higher slip angle equates to greater drag. Turning the steering wheel as little as possible is a key to fast times. (Photo Courtesy Bryan Heitkotter)

Slip Angle

Cornering Force

Drag

Force Generated by Slip Angle

The slip angle is the difference between the direction the tire is rolling (blue) and the direction the tire is traveling (green), The slip angle generates a force perpendicular to the direction the tire is rolling (orange). This force has components that turn the car (green) and slow the car (red).

Sliding this much is clearly not the fast way around. The slip angles here are so large that cornering force is significantly reduced. To compound the problem, the slide causes a significant drag force on the car, slowing it down. (Photo Courtesy Bryan Heitkotter)

As a car corners, weight is transferred. This car appears to be slowing down and turning right. Notice the difference in weight on the tires. The left front tire is heavily loaded and the right rear is barely touching the pavement. The left front is doing all the work and the right rear is simply holding the car up off the ground. (Photo Courtesy Bryan Heitkotter)

This Honda Prelude is being driven hard. The left front tire is heavily loaded and, with its large friction circle, is providing a lot of cornering force. The right rear tire is barely touching the pavement, making its friction circle a dot. Accordingly, it offers little, if any, contribution to cornering. (Photo Courtesy Bryan Heitkotter)

If the driver of this Neon mashes the accelerator, the right front tire will lose traction. The weight transfer due to cornering has made the friction circle under the right front tire very small. This small size means the tire can't accelerate much. Significant throttle application will only result in smoking this tire. (Photo Courtesy Bryan Heitkotter)

about the friction circle is that if you're not on the edge of the circle, the car is being under used.

The friction circle is normally shorter in the direction of accelera-tion than it is in braking. This is due to two characteristics of cars: (1) Two-wheel-drive cars that are set up for autocross cannot accelerate with as much vigor as they can brake, and (2) cars generally do not have enough power to accelerate at the threshold of traction (on the verge of spinning the tires) though they commonly have enough braking force to

Every force applied to a car causes weight transfer. Weight transfer changes the amount of grip a tire has and, thus, the handling balance of the car. With the right front tire completely off the ground, it isn't contributing any grip. (Photo Courtesy Bryan Heitkotter)

A sliding tire has less grip than a rolling tire. While this car has completely locked the right front wheel and is working on flat-spotting the tire, a wheel doesn't have to be locked to be "sliding." A tire that is turning at 10 mph while the car is going 35 mph experiences a similar loss of grip. (Photo Courtesy Bryan Heitkotter)

brake at the threshold of traction (locking a wheel.) As a result, the friction circle generally looks like an apple with a rather flat top.

Before you get too comfortable with the friction circle and the amount of traction that is available, remember that the friction circle is constantly changing. The circle looks different at the end of a run than it did at the beginning of that run because the tires are hotter. It looks different if you've driven into the marbles (the rubber and sand that builds up at the edge of the racing line) than it does if you've stayed on line. It's always changing slightly. Understand the concept and use it to your advantage, but don't get caught up in the numbers.

Weight Transfer

Remember how the friction circle can be applied to each tire? Think of the friction circle as we discuss weight transfer.

Increasing weight on a tire increases the amount of grip that it has on the pavement. Decreasing the weight reduces the amount of grip that the tire has. When you transfer weight by accelerating, braking, and cornering while driving around the course, you are changing the amount of grip that each tire has. You are not changing the amount of mass that this tire needs to move in order to run the car. This means that when you brake and shift weight forward, you are effectively increasing the size of the friction circle for the front tires while simultaneously reducing the size of the friction circle of the rear tires. The implications of this are huge.

When braking, the front tires have more grip and the rear tires have less. This makes the car less stable and helps it rotate. Similarly, it helps the front end of the car apply more braking force. When accelerating, the opposite happens. The rear tires have more grip. This stabilizes the car and allows the driver of rear-wheel-drive cars to apply more throttle. Reading between the lines, it also implies that you need to gently roll onto the throttle and gently apply the brakes in order to get the most out of the car.

Braking

There are several different techniques that fall into the realm of braking. Braking can be done with maximum effort, stopping the car as quickly as possible. Braking can be done with finesse to scrub a moderate amount of speed. Braking can be done without using the brakes at all, as a lift of the throttle. Regardless of why you're braking, the brake should be applied smoothly and, since the goal is going fast, braking should be kept to a minimum.

Braking for maximum effect usually happens in two different places, either before a slow corner or after the finish lights. When braking as hard as possible, the friction circle tells you that you can't generate much cornering force. So, all heavy braking should be done while driving in a straight line.

When braking heavily, how you use the brake pedal is dependent upon whether or not your car is equipped with anti-lock brakes (ABS). If the car is equipped with ABS, the brake pedal should be pressed firmly and held steady. The car will modulate the braking force to prevent brake lockup if required. If the car is not equipped with ABS, the driver needs to modulate the braking force to prevent brake

After the finish line, the driver has only one task: Slow the car as quickly as possible while maintaining control. The first part of that is being on the brakes as quickly as possible after the finish line. Autocross courses are typically designed with adequate, but not generous, finish chutes. (Photo Courtesy Bryan Heitkotter)

The second part of what needs to happen after the finish is maintaining control. The cones marking the finish chute usually count toward penalties. A driver needs to be able to safely negotiate the finish chute. In this case, the driver would have likely been better served by partially releasing the brakes to make this turn. (Photo Courtesy Bryan Heitkotter)

The cones after the finish are often referred to as "stupid cones." After the finish line, it doesn't matter how fast or slow a car is traveling as long at it is being slowed and is under control. Loss of control, even in understeer, as shown here, can only add penalties to the time. (Photo Courtesy Bryan Heitkotter)

lockup. This is known as threshold braking. A locked wheel doesn't stop the car as quickly as a wheel that is rolling.

So, drivers of cars without ABS need to be vigilant to prevent brake lockup. Two characteristics of braking systems help you understand how to prevent brake lockup. Front axles generally apply more than 50 percent of the total braking force. A tire with little weight on it locks easily. This leads you to three guidelines: One, brake gently at first to transfer some weight to the front axle and then roll onto the brakes heavily. Two, brake with the car "flat" on the pavement and all wheels loaded with about the same force. Finally, the driver needs to release the brake pedal somewhat if brake lockup is felt.

The Flat Spot

Tires are supposed to be round. A tire that is locked under braking will often not be round anymore. When a wheel is locked, the tire is dragged across the pavement. The driver notices a loss of braking force. Spectators notice smoke billowing from the tire. The tire notices a cheese grater feeling on one spot. That one area of the tire is literally getting ground off.

For cars without ABS, this is a real problem. As we drive around the course, wheels get light and lock up under braking. It is important for the driver to release the brakes and stop the lockup. (Obviously if you need to stop, stay on the brakes!) A tire that is locked long enough develops a real flat spot. The car will go "thump, thump" down the course and the wheel will lock at that same spot in the future. Beyond those two immediate troubles, a really bad flat spot can wear all the way through the tire to the nylon cords and steel belts.

So, for comfort, performance, and tire life, drivers of non-ABS cars need to be attentive to brake performance and brake lockup.

Driving a car at its limit is important to fast times. Even a small drop in cornering force translates to a significant increase in run times. A quick jerk of the steering wheel doesn't usually help the car turn. It usually results in a loss of grip. Being smooth through the corner helps keep the car at maximum grip. (Photo Courtesy Bryan Heitkotter)

Gently dragging the brakes is an effective tool to slow the car slightly for the next corner. When dragging the brakes, the car can still corner. However, the weight transferred because of braking often makes the car less stable. For this reason, it is still recommended to drag the brakes in a straight line until you are comfortable with the car and its behavior.

Lifting off the throttle is similar to dragging the brakes. There are two key differences: Lifting off the throttle offers less braking force, and lifting off the throttle applies a braking force in different proportions than actually pressing the brake pedal. The first is obvious, but the second needs to be explained. The brakes of a car are applied to all of the wheels in proportion to how the brake fluid is split by the proportioning valve in the brake master cylinder. When lifting off the throttle, the engine braking force is applied only to the driven wheels—the rear axle of a RWD car, the front axle of a FWD car, and all four wheels of an AWD car. This difference in how the force is applied changes the way a car behaves in a lift throttle situation, as compared to a braking situation. Because of this, lifting off the throttle in a corner should be done with caution.

Cornering

Cornering is easy! Look where you want to go and turn the wheel.

When it's time to go...it's time to go! Accelerating out of a corner should be done as energetically as possible without losing control. The driver shown here is probably using a little more throttle than is necessary. The car traveling sideways and the drive wheel spinning isn't quite as fast as being "hooked up" coming out of the corner. (Photo Courtesy Bryan Heitkotter)

The trick to cornering is driving the car at the limit of adhesion and as smoothly as possible. A car has only so much grip to offer. A smooth driver can approach this limit without stepping over the line. An erratic driver alternates between asking too much of the car and asking too little. As neither of these cases is optimal, the smooth driver is often faster.

The first thing to know about being smooth is that a car can't instantly go from a straight line to its maximum g-loading. Trying to do this (turning the wheel quickly into a corner) causes the tires to lose traction. Instead, drive the car in a spiral path, building cornering force as it travels down the course. Similarly, a car can't go from maximum cornering loads to a straight line in an instant—a spiral must be driven at corner exit as well. This concept is covered in depth in Chapter 3 about the racing line.

The other key concept is that the steering wheel position may need to be adjusted while cornering. Conditions change and the driver always needs to be ready to correct. Each adjustment of throttle or brake position generally requires an adjustment of steering position. A change in pavement condition also requires an adjustment of steering position. The smooth driver makes these adjustments without any quick movements of the steering wheel, helping to keep the car from jerking around.

Accelerating

How you accelerate out of a corner is dependent on how your car is driving. Front-wheel-drive, rear-wheel-drive, and all-wheel-drive cars all respond differently to the throttle. Regardless of how your car behaves, accelerate with as much vigor as possible without driving off line or upsetting the car.

In a nutshell, maximum acceleration is achieved by putting the drive wheels right at the brink of wheelspin. Spinning tires, smoking or not, are not efficiently applying power. What may strike you is that all-wheel-drive cars have a distinct advantage here. It is true that all-wheel-drive cars accelerate much better in a straight line. The next obvious realization is that rear-wheel-drive cars are better at accelerating than front-wheel-drive cars. Depending on the weight balance of the car, this is usually true. It is certainly true for well-balanced and well-set-up cars.

Any discussion of autocross and accelerating out of corners needs to address differentials. Differentials are more important to autocrossers than track drivers. Autocrossers are always using the lower gears, which have a bigger mechanical advantage than the higher gears, sending more torque to the drive wheels. More torque to the drive wheels means it is easier to spin the wheels. The difference between an open differential and a good limited-slip unit can be

The action of a differential can really change the way a car drives. The Honda S2000, for example, is a rear-wheel-drive car with a limited-slip differential. Even though the right rear tire is really light, the driver isn't worried about spinning that one tire. The driver is worried about spinning both rear tires. (Photo Courtesy Bryan Heitkotter)

remarkable. A car with an open differential might be smoking one tire while the car with the limited-slip differential is accelerating out of the corner.

Front-Wheel Drive

Front-wheel-drive cars are an interesting conundrum. Acceleration transfers weight away from the front

Front-wheel-drive cars are at a significant disadvantage in acceleration. Accelerating removes weight from the drive wheels, making it easy to spin the tires. A limited-slip differential helps quite a bit, but the front tires are still doing all the work. (Photo Courtesy Bryan Heitkotter)

tires, reducing grip for acceleration and cornering. On the other hand, the thrust that is delivered by the drive axle can be directed by the steering wheel to help pull the car out of the corner.

Front-wheel-drive cars make the greatest use of the front tires. These tires have the responsibility of doing the majority of the braking, turning, and accelerating. As can be expected, accelerating in a front-wheel-drive car is all about managing the grip in the front tires.

As the throttle is applied, the front end of the car wants to be pulled in the direction that the front tires are pointed. As more throttle is applied, the driver feels the car pulling out of the corner—until the front tires become overworked. At that point, the car begins to understeer, and one of two things must happen to stop the understeer: (1) The steering wheel must be straightened, or (2) the throttle position must be reduced.

Front-wheel-drive cars not equipped with limited-slip differentials are prone to wheelspin. The differential can't transfer torque from the spinning front-inside wheel to the gripping front-outside wheel. The driver needs to respond by lifting the throttle.

Rear-Wheel Drive

Rear-wheel-drive cars make efficient use of their tires. The front tires can turn the car while the rear tires can apply power. As a bonus, weight transfer moves weight onto the drive wheels! The only downside compared to front-wheel drive is that the thrust provided by the drive wheels is always directed straight ahead.

When applying throttle in a rear-wheel-drive car, there are a few predictable outcomes. The car can

It is fun to lay two black stripes on the pavement, but it isn't fast. Even though rear-wheel-drive cars enjoy weight being transferred onto the rear tires during acceleration, they still suffer from wheelspin. Particularly with high-horsepower cars, acceleration is an exercise in throttle modulation—how much can you give it? (Photo Courtesy Bryan Heitkotter)

drive out of the corner like it's on rails. The rear wheels can push the car straight ahead through the grip of the front tires. The rear wheels can be overpowered by the throttle and break loose, allowing the back end of the car to swing wide (oversteer). Or, as is sometimes the case for an open differential, one rear wheel spins freely and the car drives almost as if the throttle was never applied.

Regardless of how the car is behaving, the best way to apply throttle in a rear-wheel-drive car is to slowly roll onto the throttle until the car starts to lose grip. As the car starts to lose grip, ease gently off the throttle until the car regains traction. Then roll back onto the throttle. None of these movements are necessarily all-on or all-off, and the throttle should never be treated like a switch.

All-Wheel Drive

All-wheel-drive cars are a bit of a mixed bag. A lot of power can be put to the ground, but the front tires are still heavily used. Depending on the bias of the center differential, any of the front-wheel-drive or rear-wheel-drive responses are possible. All-wheel-drive torque bias can vary widely from car to car. Some cars have a static 50/50 split between front and rear torque. Some cars have a heavy front bias for torque, bordering on being fully front-wheel-drive. Some cars have dynamic differentials that vary the torque split between the axles. How the car behaves is largely dependent on the differentials.

The most common situation for an all-wheel-drive car is understeer when applying the throttle. Because of the nature of all-wheel drive, it is hard to change this characteristic. If this is the case, accelerating out of a corner requires patience. Apply only as much throttle as the car will allow—getting greedy will push you off line and chew up your front tires.

Regardless of what you drive, acceleration should start as soon as possible when exiting a corner. Give it as much throttle as you can, as soon as you can, to maximize corner exit speed. Being gentle with the throttle as it is applied or reduced helps keep the car from being upset.

Feeling the Car

Knowing what input is correct at any given moment is about feeling what the car is saying and anticipating

It doesn't matter how the weight gets transferred, all-wheel-drive cars always have all the weight on the drive wheels. The difficulty for all-wheel-drive cars comes from the differentials. One tire in the air can result in wheel spin if the differentials aren't set up properly. (Photo Courtesy Bryan Heitkotter)

Even an all-wheel-drive car can have problems. When conditions are slippery, high-powered all-wheel-drive cars can overpower the pavement and spin all four tires. Similarly, all-wheel drive doesn't help a driver brake or corner. Overall, however, all-wheel drive is a significant advantage when the pavement is slippery. (Photo Courtesy Bryan Heitkotter)

Slick conditions, such as a downpour, make the driver's job very difficult. The line between being in control and sliding becomes blurry and the car's feedback becomes muted. With the car's slower response to driver input, the driver must be quicker to make needed adjustments. (Photo Courtesy Bryan Heitkotter)

what it will say next. Feeling the car is about using all of your senses. It's true that the senses of taste and smell are pretty much irrelevant, but the point is that you should use everything available to you. A driver's shoes should be soft and flexible to adequately feel the pedals, and gloves, if worn, should be chosen with sensitivity in mind.

Most of this is obvious to anyone who has driven a car, but the following are a couple finer points to focus on in addition to feeling the changes of the g-forces in the car and seeing where you're going.

Tires make noise, and that sound can tell you something. Tires that are squealing loudly are usually sliding rather than gripping the pavement. On the other hand, quiet tires can be sliding as well. One common characteristic of soft-compound tires is a lack of audible feedback. Most true street tires squeal when sliding. Some high-performance tires and nearly all R-compound tires do not give a loud indication of the start of a slide. By the time these tires are squealing, it's too late to recover.

The weight of the steering wheel in your hands can help you feel what your car is doing. In a lot of cars, the amount of effort required to hold the wheel in the desired position is a great indicator of how much cornering force is being generated. In most cars, the cornering force also tries to straighten the steering wheel. When the wheel is turned too far, the cornering force is reduced and the car understeers. At the same time, the steering wheel often becomes very light in the driver's hands. Feeling this change will help you control the car.

As the level of grip reduces, because of rain or pavement with less overall grip, the driver needs to be more attentive to the subtle signals that the car gives. Each of these signals will be smaller and harder to detect. Most important to remember is that each signal will change slightly from car to car or site to site. Experience is the easiest way to learn these signals. The only way to get experience is more seat time.

When a car is cornering hard, the driver's first line of defense against losing control is feedback from the car. A driver must use all of the information available to make adjustments to throttle, brake, and steering positions in order to maintain control at the limit. (Photo Courtesy Bryan Heitkotter)

Looking ahead is a key skill in all conditions. When things get out of hand, looking where you want to go is the first step to recovery. If the car is sideways, the run is likely wasted, but recovering control of the car is important. Fewer cones hit means happier workers, fewer reruns, and less bruising of the driver's ego.

Horrible, painful understeer is still a loss of control. It is safe and easy for the driver to recover. This is why car manufacturers produce cars that understeer. Slowing down enough to make it through the corner can minimize understeer. Looking where you want to go is relatively easy. (Photo Courtesy Bryan Heitkotter)

Recovery

What do you do *after* you lose control of the car? Before you dismiss this as something that happens to lesser drivers, remember that everyone loses control once in a while. Some drivers are quicker to recover—quick enough that mere mortals don't even consider it a loss of control—and some drivers need to wait for the car to stop moving in order to recover; but we all lose control. Three things govern how you deal with that loss of control: how quickly you detect a loss of control, where your eyes go when you lose control, and what your first instincts are when you lose control.

Unfortunately, how soon you know things are going wrong is not something that's easy to improve. The best drivers in the world react faster to what the car is telling them, and are programmed to listen to the car more closely than the average driver. While you can improve both of these skills with more seat time, they're both the sort of thing that, ultimately, you've either got it or you don't.

Regardless of the type of loss of control, the result is typically the same. The car slides off course and the driver enjoys penalties, both in slower run times and in cones. The advantage of a car that understeers is that recovery is more straightforward—you hit three cones, but you're still pointed roughly in the right direction. (Photo Courtesy Bryan Heitkotter)

What you can do is work on your instincts. The first response to a slide determines whether control is regained quickly or not. The most important thing is to look where you want to go. When this is combined with the correct amount of steering and brake or throttle correction, the slide will be recovered. What exact inputs are required to recover quickly are based on what type of slide it is and what started the slide.

It's tough to call unexpected understeer a loss of control, but it is. Understeer is generally very stable and very easy to recover, which are two facts that guide automakers into designing cars that tend to understeer. Nearly every driver is able to recover from severe understeer simply by looking where they want to go and getting the car slowed down. The one unnatural thing that needs to be done is to steer less. That's right...the

Even a very forgiving car can get out of control. Big slides can result from even small errors. Higher speeds and slower driver reactions cause slides that seem to last forever. Slick conditions cause the same feeling. (Photo Courtesy Bryan Heitkotter)

At first glance, this car is totally out of control. But, that's not quite the case. The driver has turned into the slide and looked in the direction he wants to go, still guiding the car. When that failed, the driver depressed the clutch and brake pedals fully, locking all four wheels. (Photo Courtesy Bryan Heitkotter)

car isn't turning as well as you want so you straighten the steering wheel. This reduces the slip angle on the front tires and helps them start gripping again. It also helps keep the car from abruptly turning when the front end starts to grip again.

Oversteer is what you think of when you talk about losing control. When the back end of the car steps out, it is imperative to keep calm and look ahead down the course. Maybe you have been coached in driver's ed to "steer into the slide." Looking ahead forces you to do just that. How much you need to correct with the steering wheel varies widely, but looking ahead is always a good start. The other critical thing is to make more grip available to the rear tires for cornering. This comes in one of two ways: either shifting weight to the rear tires (increase the size of the friction circle) or reducing the amount of power being delivered to the driven rear wheels. Sometimes this means accelerating and sometimes this means gently lifting off the throttle.

When it has all gone horribly wrong and you've given up regain-

All hope is lost. So is the run. But, this driver is managing to safely stop his car even after the loss of control. By looking where he wanted to go, the driver had the ability to identify hazards and change the slide if he needed. He may not have been able to put the car where he wanted it, but he could pick a place that was "less bad" if he needed to. (Photo Courtesy Bryan Heitkotter)

ing control quickly, fully depress the clutch and brake and hold the steering wheel steady. This should lock all four wheels of the car and let the car slide to a stop in a straight line. If there is an immovable object in the path of the car, make an attempt to steer the car away from it. Don't stare at the light pole, curb, tree, whatever it is—look past it on one side or the other. Looking at it will cause you to drive into it. That would be bad.

DRIVING: THE LINE AND OTHER STRATEGIES

As this driver waits at the starting line, the time of the last car to finish the course is displayed on the reader board. Even with events timed to the nearest one thousandth of a second, a tie breaker is sometimes needed. The time of the drivers' second-fastest run is usually used to break ties. (Photo Courtesy Bryan Heitkotter)

The "line" is the path you intend to drive. Not all lines are equal. A driver with top-notch car-control skills can be beaten by a driver with lesser talent who drives a better line through the course. There is no perfect line for every car, but the general principles of line are the same regardless of what's being driven.

For a racer, the line is the plan for attacking the course. The line determines when you brake, where you turn, and how greedy you can get with the throttle. Everything hinges on where you want to put the car. For a novice, finding a better line usually results in saving seconds on a single run. And, the novice will find

that the better line is not only faster, but easier to drive.

There are a couple basic rules when deciding where the best line is. These should be considered fundamentals of the sport and, while they're not unique to autocross, they have far more impact on an autocross course than anywhere else. Every course walk should be taken with these things in mind.

Autocross is measured in elapsed time. It's a simple idea, but often forgotten. Autocross is about the quickest time between the starting lights and the finish lights. Walking a course with this in mind will open your mind up to lines that are tighter,

but travel less distance. These tighter lines often result in driving slower, but needing less elapsed time in a given course segment.

Put yourself in a position to be aggressive. This one seems easy, but it's often forgotten in the name of being aggressive. The temptation is to want to drive as fast as possible, approaching a corner and braking at the last possible second, just barely making it around the corner. Because autocross courses are so tight, there is little room to maneuver the car before the next corner. This can really punish a greedy driver with three or four corners of frustration.

HOW TO AUTOCROSS

This driver is primed and ready to attack the next section. Looking ahead down the course, there isn't any room for error—the next three corners are coming up quickly! (Photo Courtesy Bryan Heitkotter)

Putting yourself in a position to be aggressive means focusing on where you want to be at a corner exit so you can attack the next corner. It is a conscious decision to give up a little bit in one place to gain a little bit in another. Because of the nature of autocross, the little bit that is gained is usually measured in seconds while the little bit that was given up is measured in tenths of a second.

Corners

There are three ways to describe a line through a corner: geometric apexes (or "normal" apexes), early apexes, and late apexes. What's an apex? The apex of a corner is the point at which the car passes closest to the inside of the turn.

A normal apex line places the apex at the natural point for the widest radius curve that can be driven through the corner. An early apex line places the apex earlier in the corner than the normal apex. The late apex line delays the apex until after the point of the normal apex.

Turning movements are broken into three sections: the entry spiral, the central curve, and the exit spiral. The spirals occur because a car smoothly builds centripetal accelera-

It is easy to see where this driver made his apex. Being tight on the apex is a key to fast times, though perhaps this line is a tad tighter than it should have been. If the cone remains standing, this was a good line. (Photo Courtesy Bryan Heitkotter)

This driver is momentarily straight at the exit of one corner and the turn-in point of another. The rubber left by other cars shows the preferred line, gently arcing into the next apex. (Photo Courtesy Bryan Heitkotter)

tion when entering a corner (see sidebar: "Centripetal Acceleration"). This happens as the driver smoothly turns the steering wheel into the corner and the car starts to respond. The path that the car travels during this transitional period is a spiral. The exit spiral exists for a similar reason as the driver unwinds the steering wheel. The different apex lines are created by changing the entry and exit spirals, as well as the radius of the central curve.

So, that's the technical description of a corner. What, practically speaking, is the difference between the various lines? The difference lies in when the car needs to brake, when the car is able to accelerate, and how slowly the car needs to be going at any point in the corner.

The normal apex line uses the widest central curve possible. The normal apex line uses symmetrical entry and exit spirals and the widest central curve that can be squeezed into the course. This line requires the least centripetal acceleration and, thus, allows the greatest minimum speed of any line through the corner.

As illustrated in Fig. 1, the early apex line is shown as the blue dashed line. An early apex line uses a

This driver fared much better negotiating the same corner as the Nissan 350Z in the photo to the right. The choice of a later apex leaves this driver with the ability to be accelerating out of the corner and looking ahead to the next one. (Photo Courtesy Bryan Heitkotter)

Based on this driver's position at corner exit, it seems apparent that an early apex line was used. At this point, the driver is left with nothing to do but slow down and recover the racing line. (Photo Courtesy Bryan Heitkotter)

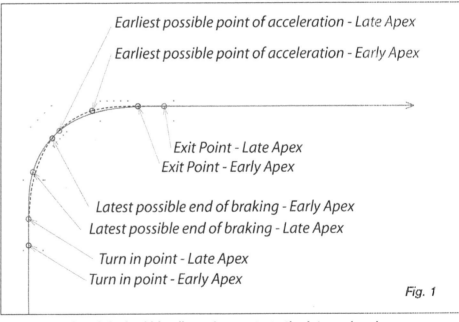

Fig. 1

The solid red and dashed blue lines demonstrate the late and early apex approaches to a corner. Note how the early apex line struggles to exit the corner while the late apex line is on the throttle early. Also note that the late apex line requires braking early and effectively prohibits any serious trail braking.

long entry spiral. Because a longer entry spiral requires less cornering effort early in the corner, the early apex line allows a driver to carry more speed into a corner than the normal apex line allowing very late application of the brakes. The long entry spiral has its consequences, however. This approach to corner entry requires a tighter central curve, requiring the driver to slow more than in the normal apex line.

To compound the issue, the exit spiral is also shorter than in the normal apex line. This means that the driver on the early apex line is still cornering rather heavily as he or she approaches corner exit. The heavy cornering demand near corner exits forces drivers to wait to apply throttle until the car is nearly out of the corner. The early apex line can be useful for road racers who are trying to overtake a rival, but autocrossers aren't passing other cars.

The late apex line is shown as the red dashed line in Fig. 1. A late apex line uses a short entry spiral. Where the early apex line allowed the driver to carry more speed into a corner than the normal apex line, the late apex line requires a slower speed at corner entry. The central curve is similar to that of the early apex line and mid-corner speeds are comparable. The payoff for the late apex line is the long exit spiral. The long exit spiral allows the driver to apply throttle very early, as compared to both the normal apex and early apex lines. The early application of throttle results in greater corner exit speeds and greater speeds all the way to the next corner. One interesting footnote to the late apex line is that,

Centripetal Acceleration

We all know that tighter corners must be driven more slowly than wide corners. The reason is centripetal acceleration–the "g forces" we feel when driving around a corner. The specific relationship between corner radius, speed, and lateral acceleration has been known for years, but it doesn't seem to be common knowledge to autocrossers.

Leaving the physics derivations to the textbooks, the relationship is $a=v^2/r$ (where a = acceleration; r = radius; and v = velocity). Very simple and easy to understand. Now, let's apply it. How fast can you drive around a 200-foot-diameter skid pad with a maximum lateral acceleration of 1.0g? Wait, that's not what we care about! How long does it take you to drive around the 200-foot-diameter skid pad? That's the right question!

$a=1.0g=32.2ft/s^2$
$r=D/2=100$ ft
$v=sqrt(a*r)=3220$ ft$^2/s^2$
$v=56.74$ ft/s (38.7 mph)

The circumference of a circle is equal to pi times the diameter.

$L=pi*D=3.14*200$ ft$=628$ ft
$t=L/v=628ft/56.74ft/s$
$t=11.07s$

It takes 11.07 seconds to drive around the skid pad. While this number is completely meaningless, let's look at what we can learn from changing parts of the example. What if the acceleration were increased to 1.1g? What if the diameter of the skidpad were reduced by 10 feet?

For 1.1g, $v=59.51ft/s$ and $t=10.55s$

Wow! Increasing the grip and maximum acceleration to 1.1g saved you half a second!

For D=190 feet, $v=55.31ft/s$ and $t=10.79s$

The corner was tighter, so you slowed down. But... you saved almost three tenths of a second. It may seem odd, but it's true. The shorter distance traveled outweighed the advantage of reduced speed.

Centripetal acceleration, applied by the tires, is what drives a car around the corner. In the car, you feel like you are being pushed toward the outside of the corner (centrifugal force). The distance between the weight of the car and the tires causes weight transfer and, in this case, body roll. (Photo Courtesy Bryan Heitkotter)

by the very nature of the line, the late apex line does not favor trail braking (where the brakes are used beyond the entrance to a turn and are gradually released up to the point of apex).

Which line is preferred varies from element to element. As a general rule, however, the early apex line is not preferred except in rare instances. This is true for two reasons: The early apex line results in the slowest corner exit speed, and the early apex line offers no margin for error if the corner is misjudged. The normal apex line has the advantages of the highest mid-corner speed, but those advantages are often outweighed by the greater corner exit speed allowed by the late apex line.

Recognize there are more than three lines through a corner. Early and late apex lines have a nearly infinite number of variations that can be driven through a single corner. Often the discussion of best line comes down to "How late of an apex do I want?"

Slaloms

Slaloms are a critical part of autocross courses. It is not uncommon to spend a full one-third of the time on course driving in slalom-like elements. Slaloms are a series of very closely linked corners. It's like driving zigzag. None of the corners are very long, but their close spacing makes car placement critical. Slaloms are all about being in a position to be aggressive and maintaining your speed.

When autocrossers talk about slaloms, they use terms like "early" and "late." These terms are commonly used to describe whether a driver is ahead of the course (early) and able to attack, or behind the course (late) and struggling to stay on course. Unfortunately for the novice, these descriptive terms mean the opposite of early and late apexes. Don't get confused.

Fundamentally, driving a slalom is about getting the front end of the car around the next cone. Drivers who hit slalom cones with the side of their car do suffer the wrath of the cone penalty, but they are often driving a good line. The driver who hits a slalom cone with the front bumper is really struggling. One way to see the line through a slalom is to try to run over the back corner of the cone with your back tire.

The proper speed through a slalom is relatively easy to figure out. A driver's speed should not vary dramatically through a slalom, but it is important to make speed adjustments if necessary. The sooner a needed speed adjustment is made, the less time will be lost. If you are worried about hitting a cone with the front of the car or feel like you're struggling to get around the cones, slow down a little. If you have a moment of leisure between cones, speed it up a little.

It is difficult for beginners to see that they are falling behind the course early in a slalom. Beginners often get behind in a slalom and fail to slow down. This is the equivalent

This driver is at the third slalom cone. The car is already around the cone and turning hard toward the next cone. The driver is in a good position to start turning back early and keep things going well. (Photo Courtesy Bryan Heitkotter)

Right on time. As the car approaches the fourth slalom cone, the driver is already working on getting around the fifth cone. The steering wheel is turned and the car is already leaning. (Photo Courtesy Bryan Heitkotter)

This driver is still doing well. The fifth slalom cone was successfully negotiated and the last slalom cone is in sight. If the course layout opens up after the slalom, the driver can be on the throttle already, accelerating down the course. (Photo Courtesy Bryan Heitkotter)

A little error at the beginning of the slalom can cause real trouble. The driver in the photo above is just a little bit late starting the first movements of this slalom. A correction now would make life much better. (Photo Courtesy Bryan Heitkotter)

It doesn't appear that a speed correction was made after getting around the first slalom cone. As the driver reaches the second cone it is obvious to the trained eye that things are starting to go badly. The driver is at the next cone and has just barely started to turn around it. (Photo Courtesy Bryan Heitkotter)

Now, with the situation becoming very difficult, the driver is slowing down. Note the slightly nose-down attitude of the car. The driver has fallen so far behind the slalom cones that a speed correction is required to make it out of the slalom safely. Had there been a correction back at cone #1, the driver could be accelerating out of the slalom. (Photo Courtesy Bryan Heitkotter)

of driving an early apex line. With each passing cone, the apex gets earlier and earlier. They have to slow down a little bit more to get around the next one. By the end of a long slalom, they've given up a bunch of time and are going very slow. It's an easy trap that every autocrosser has fallen into.

The secret to slaloms is to remember to put yourself in a position to be aggressive around the *next* cone. This happens by looking ahead and staying ahead of the course. When you get to the cone, you've already done all the work to get around it. You're looking at the next cone and already turning to get around it. When you get to that cone, repeat for the next cone.

The Slow Corner

Remember that autocross is measured in elapsed time? That's most important to remember in the slow corners. While slow corners are often a small part of the distance of an autocross course, they are a large part of the time spent on many autocross courses. More importantly, because you're traveling slowly, every extra foot that you drive costs you a lot of time. The fastest line through a slow corner is most closely tied to the shortest distance through the corner.

When walking a slow corner, pay careful attention to the apex. While most corners are driven with corner exit speed in mind, distance traveled needs to be a primary concern in slow corners. A common characteristic of slow corners is that they are tight and long. It is impossible to drive a late apex line in 180-degree corners without adding distance. The later the apex, the greater the added distance. Unless the corner is followed by a long straight and the course design, or car setup, or course conditions make it difficult to accelerate in any meaningful way out of the corner, the shortest line is quicker. If there is significant difficulty accelerating, there is likely some merit to driving a line that maintains a higher speed through the corner, even if it requires more distance.

No one likes it, but the best way through the slow corners is to slow the car down.

Making Straights

A "straight" in autocross is a relative thing. With the nature of the sport precluding long sections that are truly straight, drivers have to find a way to use the throttle vigorously. If you've heard the term "Miata Straight," this is what we're talking about—a section of the course that doesn't require slowing down to navigate the little wiggles. Not every course has these sections, but they do exist. Making the most of them can shave a few tenths of a second.

There's no hard-and-fast rule about what makes a straight. The term Miata Straight comes from the car's characteristically good handling but low power. There are a lot more Miata Straights than there are Corvette Straights because a Corvette accelerates quicker between the corners. Either way, the concept is the same: Figure out where you can be aggressive and leave the accelerator pegged to the floor.

Making straights happens in two parts. When walking the course, identify sections of the course that might allow continuous acceleration. Consider how to extend the section with minimum risk of sliding off line. If you find a section that you think you can drive very aggressively without penalty, this is your potential straight.

Once you've identified the potential straight, consider the line with

This photo shows a rather sedate Boxster. When it gets slow and tight, smoothly driving the shortest distance is the best policy. A wide line in this corner might cost a driver several tenths of a second. Getting sideways could easily cost more time. (Photo Courtesy Bryan Heitkotter)

The driver of this Celica has overdriven the entrance of this tight corner. With that mistake made, the time ticks by. The driver has to slow down and get back on line before continuing down the course. An error like this one can cost a driver a full second. (Photo Courtesy Bryan Heitkotter)

While this section of course is clearly not straight, you need to find a way to keep the accelerator down. A minor variation in line at the beginning of this section may make it easier to drive. Easier usually means faster. (Photo Courtesy Bryan Heitkotter)

full-throttle acceleration in mind. This means being willing to modify the line slightly and considering the consequences. Don't force something to be a straight if it's not one. Sometimes what looks like a straight will turn out not to be and attempting it can cost much more than the potential gains. If it looks good and the straight line doesn't look as if it will push you off line, go for it!

The next step is actually driving the section full-throttle. Good luck. It takes confidence and precision to make straights out of slaloms, offsets, and wiggles.

Linking Elements

This is perhaps the most important concept in all of autocross. In autocross, few corners stand on their own. Linking elements is all about putting yourself in a position to be aggressive.

When tying a series of corners together, the idea is to maximize exit speed and minimize time in the sequence of corners. Linking elements is usually a compromise. Expect to give up something to make up something somewhere else. If it is a series of slow corners, you will want to minimize distance traveled. If the elements are a couple of fast wiggles, consider driving a little extra distance to keep from braking—particularly in an underpowered car!

Regardless of the type of elements being linked, always consider where you want to be at the end of the section. This will help you decide how to best link the corners in question.

The Important Corner

When autocrossers walk a course, they talk of key cones and important corners. Why should one corner be more important than another cor-

When trying to squeeze the last couple tenths of a second out of the course, cones are sometimes hit. This driver got a little greedy, trying to hustle through a section of the course and just clipped this cone. It doesn't matter how hard a cone is hit, just whether or not it is safe when the run is over. (Photo Courtesy Bryan Heitkotter)

This photo shows a fast section connecting to a slow corner with the use of a kink. The car is right at the kink and the driver seems to be in a good position. The fast section of the course is wide, allowing drivers lots of room to hang themselves. Paying keen attention to how one section connects to the next will help keep you on a good line. (Photo Courtesy Bryan Heitkotter)

ner? This comes back to elapsed time. There are two ways for a corner to be important: spending a lot of time in it, or spending a lot of time accelerating after it.

The first reason is pretty obvious. If you spend a lot of time in a corner, it has a lot of influence on the total elapsed time on a course. Examples of this type of important corners are

Before the Start and After the Finish

Every club has some way to indicate to a driver where the finish of the time course is located. Some clubs use tall cones; others use colored cones. This club uses colored cones and a checkered flag. A driver at this event has little excuse for driving fast after the finish line. (Photo Courtesy Bryan Heitkotter)

Everyone drives as fast as possible between the starting line and the finish lights. Other than between those two places, you need to behave as if you're driving in a parking lot. It is a matter of safety. This cannot be compromised. As a general rule, event officials are vigilant about keeping speeds off the course low and safe. If they have to remind you twice, you'll likely be packing up and leaving.

In addition to immediate safety factors, event officials are constantly concerned about public relations. Suitable sites to host events are hard to come by and any conduct that can be perceived as unsafe or disrespectful is discouraged. This includes activities that take place on the streets adjacent to the site. Event officials seem to have eyes in the back of their heads, and they do know what happens when they're not looking. Horseplay off-site has been known to result in banishment. It isn't safe and gives the sport a bad name, so it's dealt with accordingly.

In addition to all of the above preaching, there are some normal temptations to consider. Tires work better when they are warm. It may be tempting to scrub tires or otherwise warm tires between the grid and the starting line. This is discouraged and, if aggressive enough, attracts attention from the event organizers. Burnouts are generally prohibited. Everyone has cold tires on their first runs; live with it. Use tire blankets between runs to help keep heat in the tires.

The other area of concern is between the finish line and the grid. As you pass through the finish lights, you are pumped full of adrenaline. It is important to stop as quickly and safely as possible. Not every club requires a full stop in the finish chute, but it's not a bad habit. Use this stop action to mentally disengage from the course. The run is over. After stopping, proceed slowly and carefully out of the finish area. Don't spend any extra time here. Remember that there's another car coming in behind you!

If you break these rules once in a great while, you won't be alone. It's easy to forget them in the heat of battle. This is the reason why you must be so cognizant of being in control and safe when you're not on the course.

This club uses three cones and a checkered flag to designate the finish. More importantly, the flag is located in the driver's line of sight. The unfortunate thing is that the timing lights are located at the outside of the corner. An errant car could hit the lights, disrupting the event until repairs can be made. (Photo Courtesy Bryan Heitkotter)

This driver is alert. The car is barely through the finish lights and the car is already braking heavily. This is especially important when the distance between the finish and spectator areas is short. Slow down quickly and then proceed. (Photo Courtesy Bryan Heitkotter)

Even in a car like the Viper, the slow corners are important. In a powerful car, corner exit speed is less important, but speed through the middle of a slow corner is critical in every car. The slower the corner, the longer the time it takes to negotiate it. (Photo Courtesy Bryan Heitkotter)

long and slow corners. Corners that turn more than 180 degrees are usually very important. Saving distance in these corners can result in trimming several tenths of a second off a run's time. That seems like a good reason to tidy up the line.

The second reason that a corner is important is the amount of time that can be saved *after* the corner. A corner that is followed by a long straight is very important. A modest increase in corner exit speed can be used to reduce the elapsed time on the following straight. The longer the straight, the bigger the gain.

So, by combining the two ideas, the most important corner is the long, slow corner followed by a long straight. This corner is more common than it seems. By the nature of autocross courses, long straights are generally preceded by a slow corner and a lot of slow corners are long. When walking a course, identify this corner and pick a line that empha-

sizes both the shortest line and a good exit speed. This line is very important and it is often worth compromising the line through other corners to make it work.

Key Cones

Key cones are the cones that control your driving line. A corner may have 40 cones marking the edge of the course, but there are likely only three or four cones that are actually controlling the line. Paying extra attention to these cones when walking the course and choosing the line helps block out the sea of cones. Overall, a course may be marked by 300 cones, but veteran drivers often completely ignore more than 250 of them. They're part of the course, but not important.

The significance of key cones isn't so much about determining the best line as it is about making it easier to see the best line. For example,

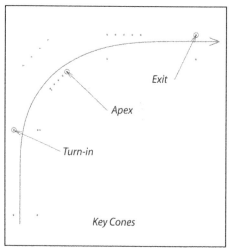

With so many cones on an autocross course, how do you know which ones to use? In this example, three cones are chosen. One cone is used to mark the turn-in point, one to mark the apex, and one to mark the exit of the corner. The other cones should blend into the background.

a slalom can be laid out many different ways. The key cones make it a slalom. The other cones marking the course are there for visual effect. A slalom can be laid out in the traditional manner—a line of cones. It can be laid out as a series of gates. It can be laid out as a C-box or series of C-boxes. In the end, only the key cones really matter.

Driving the "Swept Line"

Sometimes the best line isn't the line you want to drive. At some autocross sites, the stress of car after car being driven hard will strip sand and gravel out of the pavement. Some sites grind tires away like 30-grit sandpaper leaving behind large amounts of finely shredded rubber. Regardless of the source, these "marbles" significantly reduce grip.

When an event starts, no cars have run on the course. The entire lot looks the same. As cars drive on the lot and marbles build up, these marbles build up at the edge of the driven line. Generally, these marbles build up most heavily at the outside of corners. As the event progresses, the common line generally gets faster as the loose sand and gravel is swept away and rubber is laid down on the pavement. Just outside this swept line is all of the loose material that was swept off the line. The difference in grip level can be significant.

When a swept line is formed, it is important to follow it, whether you like it or not. The difference between being on line or in the dunes can be very small. A few inches can mean the difference between cornering hard and sliding wide. The time lost driving a less-than-optimum line pales in comparison to the time lost when sliding wide after getting into the marbles.

Driving a few events at a particular site helps you learn whether that site is prone to building up cushions of marbles. Asking a friendly local may also answer the question at a

Drifting off the "preferred" line can often result in driving in the marbles. This Acura NSX has run a bit wide in a corner and the driver has his hands full keeping the car under control. Whether it seems right or not, the swept line will have more grip. (Photo Courtesy Bryan Heitkotter)

new site. Either way, the top drivers know whether the site will build a cushion of marbles and they'll have the discipline to stay in the clean stuff.

Walking the Course

Now that I've talked at length about what to do in different types of elements, let's consider the course walk. The walk is where you have to put it all together. Unlike other forms of motorsports, autocross doesn't allow practice runs on the course. This makes the course walk critical.

Most clubs print a course map for each event. If there is a map at the registration table, take a copy. The course map can help you see where you're headed. You can use it to write down notes about the course. The map can be helpful to communicate your plan to another driver or to have them point out a critical part of their plan. If it serves no other purpose, use it to refresh your memory after the course is closed for walking.

The first walk is about reading the lay of the course. Is the course fast or slow? What types of elements are being used? Are there any "gotcha" places where it is difficult to understand where the course is going? Where are the really impor-

Quite a bit of rubber has accumulated off the racing line. In this case, a driver can afford to go a little bit off line without a significant penalty. However, the line between grippy concrete and slippery balls of rubber is very fine. (Photo Courtesy Bryan Heitkotter)

tant corners on the course? Will you need to shift gears? If possible, the first course walk should be done with a more experienced driver who is driving a similar car.

The second walk is about exact placement of cones on the course. Careful attention should be paid to key cones and apex locations. This walk should be done by walking the path that the driver's seat will travel, making the view of the cones as close as possible to what will be seen when driving the car. If you are driving a low car or a kart, squat down to see how the course looks at eye level when you're in the car. These questions should be answered on the second walk: Which corners are late apexes?

This nearly panoramic photograph shows the autocross course open for walking. At the left edge of the photo, two drivers are talking over their approach to this section of the course. With luck, they'll remember what they talked about and put it into action on the course. (Photo Courtesy Bryan Heitkotter)

Hitting cones in an F125 shifter kart is a big deal. Hitting this many cones is a really big deal. After an episode like this, a driver has to go back to the grid and think about what should be changed before the next run. Revising the line and adjusting braking points are normal adjustments between runs. (Photo Courtesy Bryan Heitkotter)

Where (and what kind of) braking is necessary? How early and aggressively can you get onto the throttle?

The third course walk is about confirming the planned line and committing it to memory. This walk can also be made with another driver if you are talking about the course. Consider this to be a critical review of whether or not your planned line is the right idea. The idea is to be fully committed to the line at the end of this walk. Right or wrong, it's what you need to do on the first run.

More course walks can be made. If more than three walks are made, it is likely that extra walks similar to the second walk are needed. That's OK. If you've got the time and need the extra walk, take it. No matter how many walks you make, the last one needs to be one of two types: a refresher of how the course looks or confirmation that the planned line is correct.

A final word about walking the course: The temptation is to be social during course walks. It's fun, but it should be discouraged if you actually care to learn the course in depth during the course walks. If any significant amount of time is spent chatting about non-course related topics, it wasn't a good walk. It was exercise, but it wasn't helpful for autocrossing.

Autocross Strategy

Drive fast! No, it's not that simple. In fact, that's not what this is about at all. Autocross strategy is about getting the most out of three runs. Some clubs offer more than three runs, but autocross is hardest when there are only three runs to get it right. If you strategize to make the most of three runs, you'll find it easy to get it right with four or five runs.

The First Run

The first run should be driven aggressively. Unless you are totally uncertain about how much grip is available or you are uncomfortable with a car's behavior, this should

Skewed Starts and Finishes

Sometimes the course designer decides to do something a little different. Sometimes the timing lights aren't placed perpendicular to the course. This skewing of the electronic eyes can change your plan about how to drive the entry or exit of the course.

First and foremost, you should try to shorten the length of the course between the starting lights and the finish lights. Autocross runs are measured in elapsed time, and reducing the length of the course is the best way to shorten a run time. This means you want to try to start on the side of the course where the lights are farthest away and finish on the side of the course where the lights are closest.

When considering the finish of the course, ponder the following. At 40 mph, shortening the course by 6 feet saves a full 0.100 second. When considering the start of the course, the speeds are slower, often closer to 10 mph. At 10 mph, saving that same 6 feet is worth 0.400 second!

The other thing to consider about a skewed start is the speed at which you cross the starting lights. It really doesn't matter how long it takes to get from the physical starting line to the starting lights. That time isn't measured. What does matter is your speed when the timer is started. This will likely be the slowest point on the course. If you can increase this speed slightly without adding distance to the course, the effort is worthwhile. It's just one more thing to consider when deciding how to line up at the starting line.

This course has finish lights that are skewed relative to the line of the course. Allowing the car to run wide at the exit of the corner makes the course longer. It becomes a trade-off: slower for a shorter course or faster and longer?

A driver enjoys one last moment of focus, and air-drying of sweaty palms, before going out on course. Finding a way to focus just before starting a run is a great way to follow the plan that was made during course walks. (Photo Courtesy Bryan Heitkotter)

be driven as quickly as possible. Drive the car fast enough to learn exactly how much grip is available. If you hit a cone, you still have two more runs to get it right. Additionally, the first run is seldom counted because second and third runs have the benefit of prior knowledge of the course at speed.

The Second Run

The second run benefits from the lessons learned on the first run and sets the stage for the third run. Now you know how much grip is available and have learned what worked and what didn't work. With this information, you can improve your position for the third run.

If the first run was clean and quick, you have options. The second run can be used to try something different—a different line or a different gear—based on something learned from the first run. Or, it can be used to drive as fast as possible.

If the first run wasn't so good, the second run becomes important. If the first run was quick but dirty, focus on making the second run clean. If the first run was slow for some reason, make a point of going faster. The second run should be used to correct any mistakes and allow you to be comfortable and confident starting the third run.

The Final Run

In a perfect world, the third run is about going as fast as you can go and not caring whether or not you hit cones. This can happen if either the first or the second run were good enough for you to live with. This means the first or second run were reasonably quick and clean. If this isn't the case, you're forced to make a "safety" run with your third run. This run is as fast as you can go without risking hitting a cone.

This driver demonstrates a nice, tight apex. Autocross is about execution and precision. It doesn't matter which run is perfect, but the goal is perfection. Job well done here, moving on to the next section of the course. (Photo Courtesy Bryan Heitkotter)

The starter indicates that the course is ready for this driver. All of the preparation comes down to putting the car into the course and getting the run that is needed. If it is the last run, the pressure is on for a fast and clean trip through the course. (Photo Courtesy Bryan Heitkotter)

There is nothing to learn on the last run. It's all about making the best run you can with what you know. If you're in a position that you don't care whether or not the run is clean, let it all hang out. The fastest autocross runs are made when there is no pressure on the driver.

Hitting Cones

How can hitting a cone be a strategy? There are two ways.

First, there is the very rare occasion when the penalty for hitting the cone is less than the time required to drive around the cone. Over the years, event organizers and course

The Weather Game

Some days the weather is uncooperative. It's either threatening to rain or it has already rained and stopped. In these cases, course conditions change rapidly during the course of a driver's runs. As such, you need to make the most of what you have.

When the weather is threatening and showers are imminent, your first run may be the only dry run. A competitive dry run is almost always faster than the best wet run. It would be a real shame to throw away your only dry run by hitting a cone. Drive the car hard, but leave yourself an extra 6 inches around the cones. If a second run can be made in the dry, it should be driven like a normal third run.

If it has already rained and the pavement is drying, the last run is usually the fastest. Pavement offers more grip as it dries. If the third run is made on the driest course conditions, it will be the fastest unless you make a mistake. All prepara-

tions should be made with this last run in mind. The car setup should be adjusted so that only easy adjustments are required to match the expected conditions on the last run, including the use of slicks instead of rain tires if appropriate. With a setup that is geared toward dry conditions, drivers need to tip-toe around the course during the early, wet runs. When the course improves, the car will be easier to drive and the driver can focus on the course between runs rather than rushing to change the car setup.

Unlike most of autocross where the driver is in control, weather is really a guessing game. Anyone who has autocrossed for a long time has been on the wrong side of changing weather. If it happens, make the best of it and try not to be discouraged.

Nobody wants to autocross in the rain. But, sooner or later, you will do it, too. Typically this results in changing course conditions. When this happens, focus is key. Every run could be the one that counts. Smooth and clean. (Photo Courtesy Bryan Heitkotter)

When the weather is really ugly, there's nothing left to do except tiptoe around the course. If you've got a spare umbrella, loan it to a course worker. There's nothing worse than working course in a downpour. Not even the timing equipment likes working in the rain. (Photo Courtesy Bryan Heitkotter)

designers have learned not to build courses with cones like these. Additionally, if this situation arises, course designers have been known to modify the course during the event (usually between run groups) to force drivers to follow the intended path. These changes usually involve adding a second cone so that a driver trying to take advantage of the situa-

tion would have to hit two cones to get the benefit. In summary, don't spend time looking for these cones.

Second, it can be beneficial to hit a cone if the alternative is missing a gate. In all cases, the penalty for missing a gate is greater than hitting a cone. Additionally, at SCCA National Tour and National Championship events, a missed gate is scored as a

DNF and no re-run can be given for any reason. If a cone was hit, a re-run can be offered later (for a timing error, red flag, or downed cone) if the need arises. If you have to choose between the two, hit the cone.

Re-runs

Re-runs are the autocross version of the Golden Ticket. It's a do-over.

A driver charges aggressively into an element. This sort of make-or-break attitude is often seen on third and final runs. If it works out, the result will be a great time. If it doesn't work out, that second run should have been a good one. (Photo Courtesy Bryan Heitkotter)

It looks as if this run isn't going to work out so well. The driver corrects in hopes that the run can be saved. Quick hands have saved many runs from the jaws of defeat. That second run is starting to look important, however. (Photo Courtesy Bryan Heitkotter)

Uh-oh. Sometimes it happens to the best of them. If autocrossers never took the chance of hitting a cone, they would never know just how fast they can go. Although this run turned out to be a loss, this driver needed to take the chance to keep himself at the limit. (Photo Courtesy Bryan Heitkotter)

It's another chance to see the course. Re-runs are given for a number of reasons, but they always result in getting to drive at least part of the course an extra time. There's not much strategy involved here except to use what was learned to your advantage.

Bumps and Other Surface Changes

Bumps and other surface irregularities can change the way you want to drive an element. The amount of grip available can change dramatically with a bump, dip, or puddle. Experienced drivers notice these items when walking the course and plan accordingly.

Autocross sites aren't smooth and flat. Some sites at airports are pretty close to flat, but even these prime sites have some irregularities. Little bumps, dips, and changes in slope can be ignored. If you're going to get the most out of your car, you need to pay attention to the larger changes in the pavement.

For years, the SCCA Solo National Championships were held at Forbes Field in Topeka, Kansas. The site's North Course was notorious for being bumpy. The pavement changes affected braking points and line. To compound the problem, water ponded in areas of the site. A key to success on the North Course was to note the important bumps and low spots.

When driving near the limit of grip, the slope of the pavement can significantly affect grip. When the pavement is falling away from you (either sloping down hill along the course or toward the outside of the corner), grip is reduced. Braking takes longer and corner speeds are reduced. If, on the other hand, the pavement is sloping up to meet you, grip is enhanced. Brakes are more

Misplaced and Downed Cones

The course isn't always set up perfectly, and course workers aren't perfect either. Even when they are perfect, sometimes safety dictates that they leave a cone down until after the next car passes. If you find a cone out of place or knocked down, you can stop for it. There are two reasons to stop for a downed cone. First, you'll get a re-run. Second, if the course workers didn't notice it before your run, they may count it against you.

The generally accepted procedure for stopping is as follows. Stop as close to the downed cone as possible without needing to deviate from the course or back up. Get the attention of the nearest course worker (you should already have this). Tell them why you stopped and point out the cone. Pointing to the cone in question will usually suffice. Proceed at a moderate speed through the rest of the course.

What is "moderate" speed? Well, there are two considerations here. If you proceed slowly through the rest of the course, you may find yourself being run down by the car behind you. This is a potential a safety problem and will likely result in a red flag and a re-run being awarded to the driver behind you. If this is one of your competitors, you

Here's a case of desperate hope: This driver is reversing to make sure he completes the course without missing a gate. Missing the gate usually means that there is no possibility for a re-run due to problems later in the run, like a red flag or timing problems. However, if reversing causes course workers to stop the next car because of safety, a DNF will be scored anyway. (Photo Courtesy Bryan Heitkotter)

don't want this to happen. On the other hand, proceeding at full speed gives you a competitive advantage over your competitors. Most clubs do not grant a re-run if you drive the rest of the course at full speed.

The magical finish line. After a successful third run, a driver can relax and start preparing for whatever comes next. It could be a work assignment or the trophy presentation. (Photo Courtesy Bryan Heitkotter)

Stock Miatas are known for showing some body roll, but this is ridiculous. Not all of the gap between the tire and the fender is roll. The car is very light after cresting a little bump in the pavement. A driver needs to anticipate these moments and plan ahead. Grip after the bump is significantly less than it was right before the bump.

effective and gravity increases your grip in the corners. The fastest drivers adjust their driving to accommodate the changes in slope.

Bumps, dips, or puddles also reduce grip. Bumps and dips are temporary problems, affecting a small portion of the course. A puddle will reduce grip for a long way, as water will be splashed out of it onto more of the course. Understand that grip in these areas will be

Once you launch from the starting line, you won't see obstacles that are off course. This event has several light poles and porta-potties within close proximity to the course. Paying attention to these items during the course walk can help you understand if there are any places that you should think about driving well within your limits. (Photo Courtesy Bryan Heitkotter)

less than it was elsewhere on the course, and plan to drive accordingly on your first run. If the bump isn't a real problem, increase your speed on later runs.

Risk Versus Reward

Sometimes it pays to drive conservatively. If you walk a course and find a place that seems likely to be a problem, drive accordingly. You could drive faster, but the reward may be small when compared to the risks. This applies when considering time lost because of a mistake. More importantly, this should be considered when the course has minimal runoff space.

When thinking about risks and rewards on course, ponder how the event has gone so far. If you have a

good run already recorded, perhaps one good enough to finish second, you can risk hitting a cone or sliding off course to try to take first place. If you don't have any good runs yet, don't risk hitting a cone to shave one more tenth of a second. Of course, if you don't care whether you finish second or seventh, you're not really risking anything by making a banzai run in hopes of winning!

As a driver you should be most concerned with what happens between the cones. Sometimes, however, certain features outside the cones cause you to change your driving habits. A course can meet the safety requirements and still present hazards to competitors. Whether the hazard is a curb, ditch, or light pole, you should do your best to avoid it. If the course design leads you to be

uncomfortably close to such a hazard, you should consider driving well within your limits in this area. This is especially true if you can't financially afford an accident. One last note: If you feel an autocross course is unsafe, talk to the organizers. If you feel uncomfortable, there is no shame in withdrawing from the event.

Once you strap yourself into a car to make an autocross run, you're not going to notice these risks. The adrenaline is going and you just won't see them, but you must be conscious of them during course walks. Make these high-risk areas part of the plan on how to attack the course. Even this technique doesn't always work. You're a driver! You don't always think about the risks once you're behind the wheel.

CAR SETUP BASICS

As soon as finding the way around the course has become relatively easy, autocrossers want to know what they can do to improve their car. One book won't hold all of the information that can be said on this subject, but I'll do my best to get you started.

Let's discuss adjusting a car with four common tools. Two of these tools are available to every autocrosser and every autocross car: tire pressure and alignment adjustment. The other two are common on autocross cars and may happen to be on an autocrosser's first car: adjustable sway bars and adjustable dampers. Coincidentally, these are also the most common adjustments to be made at an event and common upgrade parts for nearly every autocross car. These items are often inexpensive, effective at changing a car's behavior, and easy to adjust in a short period of time.

Using the Tires Effectively

A car's tires and alignment set the tone for the car's behavior. Fortunately, they're also adjustable on every car on the road. While adjust-

The blue painter's tape on this car is serving a couple purposes. It is creating a legible and contrasting car number that is easy for timing and scoring to read. It is also protecting the "high traffic" areas for cone marks. Any scuffing that a cone might leave on the car will be left on the tape and peeled off after the event. (Photo Courtesy Bryan Heitkotter)

ing tire pressure and alignment may not be the cure-all for your car's needs, it can certainly help.

Tires and Tire Pressure

Fundamentally, a car's tires are what make everything happen. The tires are the only part of the car touching the pavement. They have the responsibility of starting, stopping, and turning the car, making the tires one of the most important parts of a car's setup.

Tires are complex. The way a tire behaves is dependent upon many different qualities of the tire, the wheel on which it is mounted, and the wheel alignment of the vehicle. A tire can only work well when conditions are right, but can work poorly for any one of a number of reasons. Once a tire is mounted on a car, most people only associate one adjustment with it: air pressure. Air pressure is also the one thing that every autocrosser can adjust at an event.

HOW TO AUTOCROSS

Oversteer and Understeer

These terms are often used to describe a car's behavior in a corner. When at the limits of grip, one end of the car always seems to have more grip than the other. The end of the car that starts sliding first determines whether the car will experience oversteer or understeer. When the car fails to turn as much as the driver asks, it's called understeer. When the car turns and the rear tires struggle to keep up, it's called oversteer.

The fundamental key to tuning a car is adjusting the size of the friction circles under each of the tires. Lots of different tools exist to tune a car, but fundamentally, you're adjusting the friction circle of each tire. When understeer happens, the friction circles of the front tires aren't large enough to use the entire friction circle of the rear tires. When oversteer happens, the friction circle of the front tires is more than large enough to use the entire friction circle of the rear tires.

When put that way, it seems inevitable that every car will tend to understeer or oversteer. A perfect balance is difficult to manage. It also helps illustrate why a car can oversteer at one point on the course and understeer in another location. It makes it apparent that if the car is doing exactly what you want it to do without sliding at all, you're driving too slow!

You can also use the concept to help you understand what to expect from a tuning change. If you increase the front grip but do not change rear grip, you can expect the car to be more prone to oversteer (and less prone to understeer!). If you increase the grip on all four corners, by fitting tires with more grip for example, you shouldn't expect the behavior of the car to change.

This is one of the most frustrating feelings in autocross. The driver has turned in for the corner and the car just isn't listening. The car has more grip at the back end than it does at the front. The result: heavy understeer. (Photo Courtesy Bryan Heitkotter)

The car pushes wide at corner exit. Once understeer is initiated, there's not much for a driver to do except wait. A close look at the tires shows both the front and rear tires deflecting under the cornering forces. Perhaps a little more air pressure would have been prudent? (Photo Courtesy Bryan Heitkotter)

How do you determine what air pressure to run? Unless someone else has some experience with a particular tire, you must rely on trial and error and learn from the tire's behavior on course. An air pressure that is too low results in a tire that deflects badly under cornering loads. An air pressure that is too high results in a rock-hard tire that refuses to grip the pavement. Great. That only leaves about 40 psi of adjustment to consider.

Structurally speaking, a tire acts as a moment-resisting frame when loaded laterally—a doorway without any bracing. It holds its shape only by the stiffness of its own structure. Ordinary tires rely significantly on air pressure to hold their shape. Run-flat tires have extraordinary stiffness and can hold their shape without the help of air. High-performance tires, both street tires and R-compounds (DOT-legal race tires), are stiffer than

Whether or not a tire is folding in the corner can tell you if the tire pressure is too low. Air supports the sidewalls of the tire and too little tire pressure allows the tire to deform during cornering. This left front tire is showing a little deflection but not too much. This is probably the minimum tire pressure that should be used on this car.

A driver makes a final adjustment to tire pressures before the event starts. The tires do all the work of moving the car. Careful attention to tire pressures can prevent frustration and improve times. Ignoring tire pressures can lead to unexpected results. (Photo Courtesy Bryan Heitkotter)

Tires work best when they are flat on the pavement. Unfortunately, body roll means that you can't have all of the tires flat on the pavement all the time. Negative camber is used to make the heavily loaded outside tires be flat on the pavement in a corner, but it also means that the inside tires are tipped severely. (Photo Courtesy Bryan Heitkotter)

a regular passenger-car tire but not as stiff as a run-flat tire. Regardless of the type of street tires on the car, until some testing has been done in an autocross environment, tire pressure should be set near the maximum. After a run or two, the pressure can be adjusted based on what the tire is telling you.

A tire works most efficiently when the tread of the tire is pushed into the pavement with even pressure. You can tell how evenly a tire is working by how it wears. An easy test to check the tire pressure is to put white shoe polish (or chalk) on the outside shoulder of a tire. After a run through the course, any shoe polish that has touched the pavement will be worn away. If the shoe polish on the sidewall is gone, the tire isn't holding its shape during cornering and needs more support. Give it more air! If there is still shoe polish on the outer tread of the tire, the outside edge of the tread isn't being used at all. Try lowering the tire pressure to help the tire grab the pavement bet-ter. The "perfect" tire pressure (by this method) will be found when the shoe polish is worn away right to the edge of the tread, but the shoe polish on the sidewall is untouched. It's crude, but it does work.

Most beginning autocrossers will be fighting a car that under-steers terribly. Recall that this is because the back end of the car has more grip than the front end. It is common to set the air pressure of

In all the talk about car preparation, let's not forget about car numbers and class letters. It is tough to get a fast time if Timing and Scoring can't read your numbers. This is probably the best example of bold, contrasting numbers in all of autocross. Yellow numbers on a white car, on the other hand, don't work very well. (Photo Courtesy Bryan Heitkotter)

the front tires according to the shoe-polish method—as soft as possible without rolling over—but over-inflating the rear tires to reduce grip at the back end of the car and encourage the car to rotate. The best way to do this is to increase the pressure of the rear tires a little bit each run until the desired handling (or an absurdly high air pressure) is reached. Do not expect miracles with this technique. The car will still understeer, but the understeer will hopefully be more manageable. When using this method of adjustment, be wary of using pressure significantly higher than recommended by the tire's manufacturer, as this can cause damage to the tire.

The right front tire appears to be underinflated. In this case, the driver could use shoe polish to show how far down onto the sidewall the tire is wearing. The tire pressure would be increased until the tire wear remained on the tread for the whole run. (Photo Courtesy Bryan Heitkotter)

More advanced techniques for setting tire pressure exist, but these require a special tool called a pyrometer (see "Reading Tires").

One last thought about tires to consider. When it comes to tire wear, an autocross event is comparable to several hundred highway miles. On an autocross course, the tires are the hardest working part of the car. When a car exhibits heavy understeer or oversteer, the tires wear very quickly. An overly aggressive driving style exacerbates the problem. It is advisable to monitor tire wear frequently during autocross season. Frequent tire rotation is a great way to prolong tire life. Rotating tires front to back or left to right can keep tire wear even and help the tires last a few more thousand miles.

Reading Tires

In order to get a feel for how efficiently a tire is performing, you need to "read" the tire. Fortunately, this doesn't involve a witch doctor or fortune teller. The stress of the tire touching the pavement generates heat. The higher the contact stress between the tire and the pavement, the higher the surface temperature of the tire. By carefully measuring and recording the temperature of the

UTQG and the Tire Alphabet Soup

The Uniform Tire Quality Grade (UTQG) Standards were developed by the National Highway Transportation Safety Administration to help consumers compare tires. This means that autocrossers have some information to use for selecting DOT-legal tires. The UTQG has three rating components—all of which can be used to help narrow the field of prospective tires. These components are Treadwear, Traction, and Temperature.

The Treadwear component gives an indication of how long a tire will last under normal driving conditions. A tire is placed in service for a total of 7,200 miles and its wear rate is compared with a "control" tire. The durability of a tire in this test is often an indicator of how hard the upper tread layers are in a tire (remember, the total test length is 7,200 miles!). A higher Treadwear rating indicates a

Every tire comes with the UTQG information stamped into the sidewall. The information shown includes treadwear, traction, and temperature ratings as well as the tire's size and load rating. This tire is legal for use in Street Touring classes because the treadwear rating is greater than 140. The tire size code is also rather perplexing. The shows a 205/55/R16 89V. Broken down by component: 205 is the approximate section width of the tire in millimeters; 55 is the aspect ratio— the ratio of sidewall height to section width; R16 indicates the tire fits on a 16-inch-diameter wheel.

more durable and harder tire. The principle that a more durable tire is harder is the basis for many clubs to restrict "Street Tire" classes to tires with a Treadwear rating of 140 or greater. The idea is that if a tire is softer than that, it is likely not viable for daily driver duties on the family car.

The Traction component of a tire's rating is based on wet-weather traction. The value of this test is very limited due to the nature of the testing, but it's another piece of the puzzle. This test is designed to specifically measure the sliding resistance of a tire in a straight line at 40 mph. The test does not measure the point at which lockup occurs, resistance to hydroplaning (unless the tire hydroplanes at less than 40 mph), or cornering grip. It does, however, give an indication of the grip afforded by the rubber compound in wet-weather conditions. If a tire scores poorly here, it will likely perform poorly in the rain. The highest rating in this test is "AA" with grades "A," "B," and "C" in descending order.

The Temperature component of the rating measures how well a tire deals with the heat generated by driving down the road. This should be considered a "pass/fail" test for autocross tires. If the Temperature rating isn't "A," it won't be fit for autocross.

89V is an indication of load capacity and speed capability of the tire rather than tire size. A higher number in this component means a higher load carrying capacity. This indicator seems to be assigned at random, so be sure to consult the manufacturer's table for your specific tire. Tires appropriate for autocross generally bear the letters V, W, Y, or Z.

With all of the designations on a tire, there is some variation from manufacturer to manufacturer. One company's 205 section width is another's 215. One tire's 200 Treadwear rating is another's 240. The numbers should be used to compare tires with the caveat that it's all on paper. Real results are based on what happens when the rubber meets the road.

tires on a car, it is possible to tell which tires are working the hardest. It's even possible to tell which *part* of a particular tire is working hardest.

Taking accurate tire temperature measurements requires the use of a special thermometer, specifically a probe-type pyrometer. Immediately after stopping the car, take the pyrometer and measure the temperature of the tread of the tire. Poke the probe gently into the tread and get a reading from a millimeter or so below the surface of the rubber. The surface cools off too rapidly to give accurate readings, making infrared and other non-probe type pyrometers less reliable. Take the temperature of

A tire that is run with proper air pressure and alignment looks like this. The tire thread has been work off evenly across the tire. The sidewall appears untouched. The line between "tread" and "sidewall" is typically taken to be the wear bar indicator triangles on the shoulder of the tire. The triangle should not be touching the pavement. (Photo Courtesy Bryan Heitkotter)

The use of a probe pyrometer is the best way to tell how a tire is being used. The probe reads temperatures below the surface of the tire, which is more indicative of the actual tire temperature. High temperatures indicate a portion of the tire that is working hard. (Photo Courtesy Bryan Heitkotter)

This is a closeup of nylon-reinforcing cords in a tire. As is rather common, the tire was worn out along the outside shoulder. Once cords are exposed, the tire is no longer safe to drive on. One requirement of autocross tires is that no reinforcing cords are showing on the tires at any time. Unless this driver has a spare autocross tire, his day is done. (Photo Courtesy Bryan Heitkotter)

each tire in three locations: inside shoulder, middle, and outside shoulder. Record the data. The hotter a particular band of the tire is, the harder it is working.

Pyrometer data can be used to check tire pressure and alignment. A tire that is working efficiently has nearly equal temperatures across the whole width of the tire; the higher temperatures are on the inside shoulder of the tire, and the lower temperatures on the outside shoulder of the tire. Ideally, all three bands will be within about 10 degrees of each other. Here are some quick guidelines of how to adjust a car based on pyrometer data:

- *Center of tire is hottest:* Tire pressure is too high
- *Center of tire is coolest:* Tire pressure is too low
- *Outside shoulder of tire is hottest:* Too little camber
- *Inside shoulder of tire is hottest and hotter than optimum:* Too much camber

While these guidelines aren't foolproof, they're a place to start.

Types of Tires

Autocross tires come in three distinct varieties: street tires, street-legal race tires, and true race tires. Of these three groups, true race tires are the least common. This is because few autocross classes (typically only Prepared and Modified classes) permit the use of true race tires and these classes are often less popular than other classes. Street tires and their R-compound relatives, street-legal race tires, are very common and very different from each other.

Most clubs define street tires as tires that are DOT approved for use on public highways and bear a tread wear rating of 140 or more. These are high-

Tires are the most important part of a car's performance. Without a good tire, even the highest performance sports car will be hobbled. Tires that come as original equipment on a car aren't necessarily chosen for their performance, even on a car like the 911 GT3. (Photo Courtesy Bryan Heitkotter)

Dedicated autocross tires are expensive. Since they don't wear well on the street, it is common for autocrossers to swap tires at events. This means having an extra set of wheels and the tools to change tires. It also means having all of this stuff at an event. (Photo Courtesy Bryan Heitkotter)

performance tires designed to be driven on the highway. These tires generally have relatively deep tread and wear quickly, often not lasting more than 10,000 miles on the highway. As street tires go, these tires are very sticky and the cutting edge of passenger-car technology. But, they're still designed with rain performance and comfort in mind. Most tire manufacturers make high-performance tires and, with new tires coming out all the

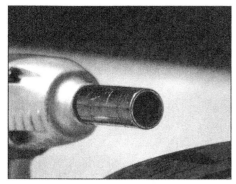

The electric drill has much improved the life of the autocrosser. The electric impact wrench has worked similar wonders. With modern tools, it is possible for a competitor to change all four tires on the car in less than 15 minutes. Of course, it does mean packing more stuff to an event.

time, a quick walk around an autocross grid is probably the best way to see what's most popular.

R-compound tires are also DOT approved for highway use, but have no minimum tread-wear rating. These tires often only have circumferential grooves and commonly have "Not intended for Highway Use" stamped into the sidewall. R-compound tires are very sticky, very soft, and wear very quickly. They do not hold up well to cruising down the freeway and might only last 1,000 miles before being worn out. R-compound tires are still a compromise, but only between performance and DOT standards. Comfort and rain performance are not generally considered in design. A few companies manufacture R-compound tires. The most prominent in the market today are Kumho and Hoosier. BF Goodrich, Yokohama, Hankook, and Toyo also have popular R-compound tires, though their competitiveness at autocross events is currently unproven. Again, asking autocrossers about the currently competitive tires is likely the most effective method of mining information.

Autocross tires work best in a very specific temperature range. If they are too cold, they won't grip the pavement very well. If they're too hot, they get greasy and slide. The use of water sprayers and evaporative cooling can keep tire temperatures in check on a hot day. (Photo Courtesy Bryan Heitkotter)

Bluntly put, the softer the tire, the greater the grip afforded by the tire. Also, the softer the tire, the shorter the life of the tire. R-compound tires are softer than street tires, don't last as long as street tires, and have more grip than street tires. Within the R-compound and street tire realms, tire hardness varies by brand and model of tire. Generally speaking, a lower tread-wear rating indicates a softer tire.

A car's alignment is very important to performance. Adjustments to camber and toe can significantly change the handling and performance of a car. This Subaru Impreza WRX has a significant amount of camber at the front end of the car, but not much at the rear. (Photo Courtesy Bryan Heitkotter)

Alignment

As was mentioned previously, tires are most efficient when they're pressed evenly on the pavement. While air pressure is part of the equation, a car's alignment is a bigger factor in how the tire is actually loaded. A car's alignment determines if the wheel is tilted relative to the pavement and how much needs to slip to roll along with the rest of the tires.

Without changing suspension parts, there are three alignment settings that may be available: camber, caster, and toe. Camber is a measure of how much the tire is tipped relative to vertical when viewed from the front or rear of the car. Caster is a measure of how much a front hub is tilted relative to vertical when viewed from the side. Toe is a measure of how close to parallel the tires of a single axle are.

Camber

Most modern cars have some camber adjustability. Higher performance cars may even have enough

adjustment with stock components to meet the needs of the average autocrosser. But don't count on it. The trend seems to be for minimal front-camber adjustment and adjustability of rear camber varies widely from car to car—some have quite a bit of adjustment; some have none.

Camber is very important to a car's performance on an autocross course. Camber has a significant impact on how well a tire performs at a given instant. Adjusting camber has the effect of changing how efficient a tire is in a given situation. Increasing negative static camber often improves cornering performance. Running near-zero static camber is generally most efficient for pure acceleration and braking. Camber is yet another compromise in performance.

The right amount of static camber is dependent upon many factors, both related to the car and to the tires and racing surface. Overall, optimum static camber for maximum grip is dependent upon a car's roll stiffness, the amount of grip the car is using, and the amount of camber that is gained or lost in suspension travel.

Camber is the amount that a tire is tipped relative to vertical. Negative camber has the top of the tire tipped toward the body of the car. In this photo, the rear tire shows visible negative camber. In a right-hand corner, the body of the car will roll to the left and the tire will be nearly vertical on the pavement. (Photo Courtesy Bryan Heitkotter)

Grip and roll stiffness combine to determine how much a car leans when cornering. For every degree that the car leans or "rolls" in a corner, the wheel and tire lean 1 degree. For a given car, roll is dependent upon grip. More grip equals more roll. The right amount of camber on dry pavement and race tires may be far from perfect in the rain.

The other key factor affecting optimum static camber is suspension geometry. When a car turns and load is transferred, the suspension of the car moves. This motion changes the geometry of the suspension. This change results in a change in

Picking the Right Helmet

When autocrossers start upgrading their car, they're usually pretty hooked on the sport. If you're hooked, step up to the plate and buy yourself a helmet. You don't really want to use the loaner helmets forever, do you? With helmets costing between $100 and $500, take a little time to pick out the right one for you.

Helmets come in two distinct styles. A full-face helmet completely covers the head and usually comes with a visor. Open-face helmets lack a chin bar and visor. Each type of helmet has its own niche and more than preference should weigh into the decision when choosing between the two styles.

Generally speaking, full-face helmets offer more protection than open-face models. It makes sense. They cover the whole head. Full-face helmets are essentially required for driving open-cockpit cars. This includes all autocross cars that lack a windshield or have a windshield that is smaller than stock. The reasoning here is eye protection and an open-face helmet can be used in these cars in conjunction with a face shield or goggles. If you plan on autocrossing one of these cars, buy the full-face helmet. Research has shown, however, that a full-face helmet may not be a good idea when combined with airbags. The danger is that the airbag will push the chin bar into the driver's chin, concentrating the airbag's force into a small area.

So, other than for cars with airbags, why would you want an open-face helmet? Open-face helmets often offer better peripheral vision. Open-face helmets offer easier communication, as your voice will be heard normally when speaking and other's voices are less muffled when listening. Open-face helmets often work better for drivers with eyeglasses. Finally, full-face helmets aren't for the claustrophobic.

After deciding whether to look at open-face or full-face helmets, you need to decide what testing standard you want. Most clubs honor Snell SA- or M-rated helmets. The SCCA allows K-rated helmets as well. Each of these standards is developed for a particular purpose. SA helmets are designed for road racers. M-rated helmets are designed for motorcyclists. K-rated helmets are designed for kart racers. If you expect to cross over into other forms of motorsports, it would be prudent to buy the appropriate helmet.

Picking out a helmet is tricky business. Likely the best opportunity to try a helmet on for size will be to borrow a friend's helmet. Aside from that, motorcycle shops typically have a selection of M-rated helmets to choose from. For K or SA helmets, you'll probably order online or over the phone. In this case, test fit a friend's helmet. Most helmets from the same manufacturer will fit the same. Those wearing eyeglasses need to be particularly wary of fitment, as not all helmets accommodate glasses. There are some size differences between brands, however. Helmets should fit snugly and the best fit will have you feeling that the chinstrap is useless.

Here are two well-loved helmets. The one on the left is a full-face helmet; the one on the right is an open-face model. The stickers on the lower left side of the helmets are often affixed during technical inspection. The sticker allows the starter to easily see whether or not the driver's helmet has met the requirements for the event.

This is the elusive Snell certification sticker. This sticker is located inside the helmet, often under the lining. This particular helmet bears an SA2000 certification. Nearly every helmet without a Snell rating will not pass a technical inspection at an event, and this sticker is the proof that the inspector is looking for. A DOT certification won't get through tech.

When performing field repairs or adjustment, safety should be considered. Place jack stands under the car before starting to work. If working on hot parts like the engine or exhaust, use gloves. (Photo Courtesy Bryan Heitkotter)

This is an example of a camber/caster plate. This device allows the person performing the wheel alignment to adjust both camber and caster on a car with McPherson struts. By moving the top of the strut left or right, camber is adjusted. By moving it forward or backward, caster is adjusted.

camber, caster, and toe. In some cars, this geometry change results in beneficial changes to tire position and in some cars it is detrimental. Cars with McPherson struts, for example, typically lose camber under heavy cornering. Cars with upper and lower A-arms, on the other hand, can be designed to gain some camber through most of their suspension travel.

Finally, camber can be used in two different ways to adjust a car's balance in a corner. It can be used to add grip or remove grip. For the understeering car, front grip should be added. To do this, change the camber so that the entire tire is worked evenly in a corner (see "Reading Tires.") This will likely mean adding camber, but not always. After front grip has been adjusted as well as possible, and if understeer is still present, it is possible to remove rear grip by intentionally making the rear tires less efficient. A similar set of adjustments can be made to a car that oversteers, adding rear grip and reducing front grip.

Caster

Caster is not commonly adjustable on stock automobiles. Changing caster modifies how much change in camber is realized when the steering wheel is turned. Positive caster is where the upper ball joint or pivot is rearward of the lower ball joint. Positive caster effectively increases the camber (makes more positive) on the inside front wheel as the steering wheel is turned. Similarly, positive caster effective decreases the camber (makes more negative) on the outside front wheel as the steering wheel is turned.

At face value, it would seem that increasing caster is always a good thing. Positive caster tilts the tires in the correct direction to counteract camber losses due to body roll. This allows the use of less static camber to maintain the same tire-to-pavement orientation at a given steering angle. Both front tires can work more efficiently mid-corner and the reduced camber affords additional straight-line grip for acceleration or braking.

Unfortunately, it's not quite that simple. There are drawbacks to large amounts of caster. As caster is increased, the driver must turn the steering wheel farther to get the same steering angle at the wheels. Increased caster may reduce the tendency of a car's steering wheel to return to center on its own. Also, high caster settings cause additional wear and tear to the ball joints locating the front hubs. On McPherson strut cars, increasing caster reduces the effective rate of the front springs.

Toe

Let's forget the definition of toe. Toe does one thing: adjusts stability of the car. Toe-in (the front edge of the tires point toward each other) makes that axle more stable. Toe-out (the front edge of the tires point away from each other) makes that axle less stable. Physically, changing toe changes the slip angle of the tires making them more or less efficient in certain situations. Every car has adjustable front toe and most cars (solid rear axle cars excepted) have adjustable rear toe.

Front toe affects how "darty" a car feels. A car with toe-in allows a driver to move the steering wheel away from center without really changing the direction of travel. A car with toe-out tries to change directions very quickly, often for no apparent reason. On the highway, toe-out is generally discouraged, as the car tends to follow every rut and change lanes on a whim, generally requiring constant attention to drive straight. On the autocross course, you're trying to change directions very quickly and you're (hopefully!) always fully focused on driving the car. As a result, it is common for autocrossers to want a little bit of front toe-out. It is also common to see autocrossers changing front toe at an event—they didn't want to drive the car that way on the highway!

A good compromise is to run zero front toe. Car manufacturers commonly specify a small amount of toe-in to make the car stable. Changing this to zero toe allows a car to change directions quickly without becoming skittish on the street.

Rear toe affects how well the back end of the car follows the front end.

A car with oversteer can be adjusted back toward neutral handling with changes to the alignment. The driver can either reduce grip at the front of the car or add grip at the rear of the car. Obviously adding rear grip is the preferred solution.

With a big slide like this, the rear tires build up a lot of heat. If the rear tires are heated too much, the car oversteers for the rest of the run. If the driver induced this slide by making an error, the car may oversteer for the entire run with a near-perfect setup. If a setup adjustment is made because of a driver error (rather than a real setup problem) the car won't get better. (Photo Courtesy Bryan Heitkotter)

Tire Wear and Alignment

Worn-out bushings and ball joints can cause odd or excessive tire wear. However, unless your car has a lot of miles on the clock, those parts aren't likely the cause. Even if they are the roots of the problem, the first step to diagnosing the issue is checking the alignment.

While camber can cause excessive tire wear, it's not usually the culprit. Small variations in camber have a negligible effect on tire wear on the highway. Camber doesn't affect how much stress a tire experiences, it only affects which part of the tire is most highly stressed. Toe, on the other hand, eats tires.

Excessive toe, either toe-in or toe-out, can quickly destroy a set of tires, regardless of driving style. Zero toe sets both tires on that axle to point straight ahead and the tires will roll relatively easily. As toe is increased, the tires are no longer pointed straight ahead and are effectively being dragged down the highway.

The worst scenario for an autocrosser is to drive around with both toe-out and lots of negative camber. The toe-out causes the inside edge of the tire to be dragged along the pavement. The camber makes the inside edge of the tire work hardest on the highway. The combination wears out the inside shoulder of the tire in short order.

If you've checked the static alignment and nothing seems amiss, the wear could be caused by worn-out bushings. When driving, worn bushings can allow the suspension alignment to change due to the loads of driving. Commonly, these stresses result in more more toe-out causing excessive wear of the inside shoulder of the tire.

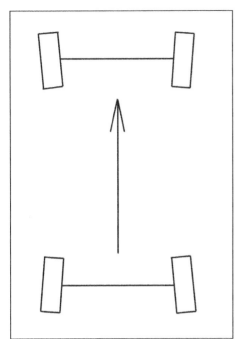

Toe describes how the wheels on an axle are pointed. In this figure, the front axle has toe-out and the rear axle has toe-in. Toe is commonly measured in both degrees (for alignments performed on a machine) and inches (for alignments done by hand).

Rear toe-in makes the back end of the car more stable, while toe-out makes the back end of the car try to pass the front of the car. Again, it is common for automakers to specify rear toe-in to make a car stable on the highway. Some cars need copious amounts of rear toe-in for stability. Some cars need toe-out just to turn. Be very careful when adjusting or specifying rear toe. A small change in rear toe can make a car that previously handled well now completely undriveable.

Adjusting Roll Resistance

The resistance of a car to leaning, or roll, while cornering is a primary factor in how a car behaves. There are two reasons for this: Roll affects how the tires touch the pavement and relative roll resistance determines how

This Mazda MX-5 is a well-set-up car. Visually, the car has enough camber to compensate for the body roll. The inside tires are tilted heavily, but the more important outside tires appear to be pretty close to vertical. (Photo Courtesy Bryan Heitkotter)

The driver appears to have turned in too soon. That cone looks to be done for. The driver is actually compensating for the time it takes the car to respond to his inputs and the amount the car is going to slide.

A well-set-up car can be driven hard at the limits of grip without any real consequences. In this case, the car slides wide of the cone (sparing the driver a two-second penalty) but doesn't seem to exhibit the signs of serious oversteer or understeer. (Photo Courtesy Bryan Heitkotter)

Some cars come from the factory with relatively stiff sway bars. This car is using the stock rear sway bar and it is clearly stiff enough to lift the inside rear tire off the ground. A stiffer front sway bar would reduce body roll, perhaps to the point that the rear tire stays on the ground. (Photo Courtesy Bryan Heitkotter)

A car's springs and sway bars are the primary resistance to body roll. Dampers are also part of the equation, especially on cars with soft springs and sway bars. Reducing body roll is important to performance. Body roll means tires don't work effectively and grip is reduced. (Photo Courtesy Bryan Heitkotter)

Big sway bars need tough mounting points. The sway bar shown here is attached to the car with a heavy-duty bracket. A sway bar that is stiffer than stock can overstress the stock mounting points and actually pull them off the car. A little research and up-front work can save headaches down the line. (Photo Courtesy Bryan Heitkotter)

much weight transferred each corner of the car will carry in a corner.

It is clear that a car's body roll influences grip by tilting the tires on the pavement, but tires are also sensitive to how much vertical load is placed on them. More load equates to more grip, but the tire is also less efficient (if the load is increased by 50 percent, the grip may only increase 40 percent.) Increasing the roll resistance of one axle of a car causes more load to be transferred at that axle, making the tires on that axle work less efficiently. It is this principle that you work with by stiffening or softening the chassis.

Sway bars and dampers are part of a car's roll resistance. They are both commonly adjustable and work in different ways to affect a car's behavior.

Sway Bars

Fundamentally, a sway bar acts as a spring that connects the two wheels on an axle. This spring is only activated when the axle is twisted relative to the chassis. If both wheels move up or down together, no sway bar force is generated. In other words, sway bars only affect roll. A car's springs offer the primary resistance to roll, but sway bars can help fine-tune the balance of a car. Also, in cars with soft springs, sway bars can help augment inadequate roll resistance without swapping out the factory springs.

Physically speaking, sway bars are a mechanical link between the left and the right springs on an axle. The most common sway bar design today is that of a torsion bar. As one spring is compressed and the other extends, the sway bar is forced to twist to allow the two springs to move in different directions. The harder it is to twist the bar, the stiffer the link between the two springs. The harder it is to move the springs relative to each other, the greater the resistance to roll motion at that axle.

The most important characteristic of sway bars is that the force in a sway bar is displacement based. The greater the difference in wheel position between one side of the car and the other, then the greater the force in the sway bar will be. Put another way, sway bars are most effective when a car is leaning heavily to one side, such as in the middle of a corner. Adjusting a sway bar will affect steady-state cornering much more than transient motions. Think sweepers.

For the average autocrosser, adjusting a sway bar is one of the most effective methods of changing a car's behavior between runs. Most sway bars are easy to adjust and have a relatively wide range of adjustment. Two different methods of adjustment are common: adjusting the stiffness of the center torsion bar section of the sway bar and adjusting the leverage between the suspension and the torsion bar section. The first

adjustment is straightforward. A stiffer center section will stiffen the bar. The second adjustment requires a little knowledge to get correct. The shorter the distance between the torsion bar and the bar endlink, the stiffer the bar will be. A third, less common, method of adjusting a sway bar's stiffness is to stiffen or soften the sway bar's arms. A stiffer arm will put more force into the torsion bar than a softer arm. These sway bars are commonly referred to as "blade"-style bars as the sway bar arms will look like a blade.

Common adjustment methods:

- On a car that can't get enough camber, increasing sway bar stiffness reduces roll and allows the tires to work more effectively.
- A car that understeers can often benefit from a softer front sway bar or a stiffer rear sway bar.
- A car that oversteers can often benefit from a stiffer front sway bar or a softer rear sway bar.

One final word about sway bars: Sway bars limit suspension travel. If

In the battle to make a car work well on an autocross course, compromises need to be made. In this case, a stiffer front sway bar might promote understeer in the corner. On the other hand, a stiffer front sway bar would help load the inside rear tire more heavily, helping to prevent wheelspin at corner exit. (Photo Courtesy Bryan Heitkotter)

The use of a stiff front sway bar can lift the inside front tire off the ground at corner exit. For front-wheel-drive cars, this would be a bad thing. For this rear-wheel-drive BMW, lifting the inside front wheel helps ensure that the inside rear wheel is loaded up as much as possible to accelerate out of the corner. (Photo Courtesy Bryan Heitkotter)

Stiff dampers don't help much in long, sweeping corners. In a slalom, however, the car is always moving back and forth. A stiffer damper can help reduce body roll in slaloms and increase responsiveness of the car at the same time. (Photo Courtesy Bryan Heitkotter)

This photo was taken at the same location as the one of the blue Acura. Notice that the Mini enjoys significantly less body roll than the Acura. Many things contribute to this, but the Acura could be this flat through the slalom with stiffer dampers. (Photo Courtesy Bryan Heitkotter)

Dampers

Dampers, or shock absorbers, are primarily used to control the motions of the wheels and keep the tires smoothly pressed into the pavement. Without dampers, a wheel that strikes a bump will keep moving up and down until friction stops the motion. We've all seen the car driving down the road with a tire that keeps bouncing. That car needs new dampers. When talking about using dampers to adjust the handling of a car, always keep the damper's primary function in mind: to keep the tires on the pavement. Going overboard with stiff dampers does not improve grip, however.

Physically, dampers use viscous friction to dissipate energy from the hub/wheel/spring assembly. A piston rests in a tube of oil. The piston is attached to the wheel. When the wheel is moved up or down, the piston is forced to move and the oil must move around the piston. The

you are having trouble with wheelspin, think about the stiffness of the sway bar on the drive axle. It is common, particularly on the back of front-heavy cars, for a sway bar to completely lift the inside rear tire off of the pavement. Clearly, it's difficult

to accelerate with one of the driving tires off the ground! More commonly, a sway bar will make a tire very light, promoting wheelspin. If you've got a heavy sway bar on a drive axle and are experiencing wheelspin, consider finding another solution.

faster the piston moves, the harder it is for the oil to move through the piston. If the wheel and piston aren't moving up or down, the damper isn't doing anything. In other words, dampers are only effective in transient motions. Think slaloms.

Most cars don't come factory equipped with adjustable dampers. That said, it is easy to find aftermarket adjustable dampers for most performance cars. Adjustable dampers come in two distinct types: off-the-shelf direct replacements for the stock dampers and high-end custom-built dampers intended for race applications. Prices vary widely. About $500 can buy a set of inexpensive off-the-shelf adjustable dampers, while $5,000 won't always be enough to buy the top-of-the-line custom-built dampers. Every damper has its own niche and purpose, but they all fundamentally function in the same manner.

In order to get the most out of an adjustable damper, it is critical to understand what the external adjustments actually do. Dampers use different pieces to make their force, depending on which direction the wheel is traveling. If the wheel is traveling up, it is called "compression" or "bump." If the wheel is traveling down, it is called "rebound." External adjusters on a single-adjustable damper (a damper having only one adjustment knob) can adjust only compression, only rebound, or both compression and rebound together. Commonly, single-adjustable dampers adjust rebound only or both compression and rebound together.

Used properly, compression and rebound adjustments are made for different reasons. Compression damping should be adjusted to compensate for a very smooth or very bumpy road surface. Rebound damping can be used to adjust the balance of

Adjustable dampers offer the flexibility of being able to adjust the stiffness without needing to disassemble the damper. This can allow a competitor to enjoy a relatively smooth ride on the street and still have the desired performance on the autocross course. Adjusters are typically mounted on either the top (as shown here) or bottom of the shock body.

a car in slalom-type elements. Adjusting compression and rebound together makes a bumpy surface feel harsher, but also stiffens the car in slaloms.

Common damper adjustment methods:

- A car that responds slowly in a slalom will benefit from more overall damping force.

- A car that oversteers in a slalom will benefit from more front damping force.
- A car that understeers in a slalom will benefit from more rear damping force.
- Adjusting rebound damping should be the preferred method of adjustment of car balance.
- A car that skips or skitters over bumps will benefit from less overall damping force.

The real comparisons between one setup and another are between two examples of the same car. This Mazda RX-8 shows a significant amount of body roll in this slalom element. It isn't horrible, but the car could be kept flatter. (Photo Courtesy Bryan Heitkotter)

Here is another RX-8 at the same location on the course. This car seems to show a little less body roll. This should let the tires work a little bit better. What is different? Likely this car is using a little stiffer damper than the first car. (Photo Courtesy Bryan Heitkotter)

All adjustable dampers are not created equal. There are three important characteristics of dampers: durability, adjustability, and damping rates. While durability should be obvious, "shock novices" often overlook the other two characteristics. Here are the first two questions about adjustability you need to be able to answer: How many steps of adjustment are there and how big is each step? It is generally advantageous to have more steps of damping force to use, but if the total range of adjustment is very small, the damper may not be terribly useful. On the other hand, a wide range of adjustment may be mostly useless if the damper only has four settings.

Finally, the damping rates are very important. How much force is created at the softest and stiffest settings? Is the damper digressive or linear? What is the ratio of compression damping to rebound damping? These are all important questions that are discussed later, but until you understand the significance of each question, you won't likely get your money's worth out of custom dampers. There are precious few shock builders that understand the nature of autocross well enough to design damping curves that are right for you without spending a lot of time driving your car. Sound advice would be to do a lot of homework before placing your order for a $4,000 set of dampers.

With all this talk about car setup, the fundamentals are still important. Nothing is more embarrassing than having parts of your car fall off while on course, but it happens. A muffler is especially tough because a course worker can't even really pick it up. The driver following might get a re-run if the debris can't be moved in time. (Photo Courtesy Bryan Heitkotter)

ADVANCED CAR CONTROL

Once the basic skills are mastered and a driver is quick on course, new skills can be learned. These skills, while not required to successfully complete the course, are necessary to truly master the sport. This mastery involves not only how to perform these skills, but knowing when to use them. (Photo Courtesy Bryan Heitkotter)

The difference between a good driver and a great driver lies in how well he or she can walk the line of control. Great drivers can brake later and accelerate earlier than the rest of us without compromising car control. (Photo Courtesy Bryan Heitkotter)

Once the basic skills have been mastered, a driver can start shaving tenths of a second with a few advanced skills. None of these techniques will shave large amounts of time, but they're all pieces of the larger car control puzzle.

Blending Inputs

The first advanced technique is to blend inputs. Previously, I discussed doing one thing at a time: brake, turn, and accelerate. It is natural to overlap these driver inputs subconsciously. Earlier advice was given to try to separate these actions as much as possible to keep the car stable and under control. With the basic skills mastered, you now have the skills to control the car while blending inputs.

You already know that the car won't respond to two significant inputs being made at the same time. The blending of inputs is done with low to moderate levels of the two actions, ensuring that the car's friction circle is not exceeded. If you strictly adhere to the "brake, turn, accelerate" sequence without any overlap of inputs, you only trace vertical and

Trail braking is the name given to overlapping braking and cornering. Trail braking is required when braking late in to a corner and is sometimes useful to help a car rotate. The process involves light braking as the steering wheel is turned into a corner. (Photo Courtesy Bryan Heitkotter)

horizontal lines on the friction circle. By blending your inputs, you can fill out the circle.

Trail Braking

Trail braking is the term used to describe overlapping braking and turning inputs. The concept is to brake absolutely as late as possible by easing off the brakes as the steering wheel is turned. This technique allows a driver to apply braking force at a time when the steering force is not using the whole friction circle.

Trail braking fills in the lower portion of the friction circle.

Trail braking can save you a small amount of time at corner entry. The technique takes advantage of grip that is not being used for turning the car by applying it to braking. The keys to trail braking are to remember that trail braking does not involve either maximum braking effort with the steering wheel turned or maximum cornering effort with the brake applied. As such, this is a very brief period of time, perhaps less than a second. The initial

braking point moves only a few feet and the time saved is measured in hundredths of a second.

The most noticeable thing about trail braking (when done properly) is that the back end of the car feels light and unsettled at turn-in. This is because you're still on the brakes at corner entry. The act of braking has transferred weight (and grip) from the rear tires to the front tires. Trail braking a well-balanced car often results in oversteer. For a car that is prone to heavy understeer, this technique may help the car rotate at corner entry. For those driving cars that are prone to oversteer, trail braking is often a losing proposition.

If, when attempting to trail brake, the car exhibits terminal understeer, the driver is asking the front tires for more than they can give. Braking forces are applied more heavily to the front tires than the rear (rightfully so; remember, weight transfers to the front under braking). When asking the front tires to both slow the car and turn into a corner, it is easy to be overly aggressive and exceed the available grip on the front tires. When this happens, the car neither turns nor stops with any

Blending of inputs asks a lot of the tires. You must remember that when cornering, the brakes don't work as well as they do in a straight line. Similarly, when braking, the tires aren't as effective at turning the car. Applying heavy brakes and turning the steering wheel sharply will result in a loss of control. (Photo Courtesy Bryan Heitkotter)

When a driver drags the brakes at corner entry, a car's weaknesses are exposed. In this case, the inside front tire is locked up. In cars without ABS, trail braking is a difficult operation. It is very easy to flat spot a tire.

This driver is looking for corner exit and, hopefully, already applying some throttle. Once the driver starts unwinding the steering wheel, the throttle can be applied. Gently at first, but with more vigor as the corner opens up onto the next straight.

Braking while cornering can lead to brutal understeer. The front tires are being asked to turn the car and slow it down at the same time. When the driver asks for too much from the front tires, the car won't slow or turn easily. Easing off the brakes and straightening the steering wheel will actually help the car turn. (Photo Courtesy Bryan Heitkotter)

Early Acceleration

This technique isn't really anything beyond just accelerating as early as possible. The only reason that it is included here is to make you think about just how early you could be accelerating. Smoothly rolling onto the accelerator as early as possible is one of the keys to fast times. When applying the throttle in a corner, patience and feel are required. It is really easy to be too aggressive.

Dragging the brakes lightly at corner entry is called trail braking. Trail braking can be a very effective method to get a car to rotate, but it needs to be done with caution. The rear of the car can get very light and make the car unstable. (Photo Courtesy Bryan Heitkotter)

Trail braking has helped this car rotate nicely at corner entry. It appears, however, that the back end of the car has lost all grip. At this point, releasing the brakes will help the situation. In all-wheel-drive and front-wheel-drive cars, applying throttle also helps a driver regain control. (Photo Courtesy Bryan Heitkotter)

Shifting

Shifting—an advanced technique? What? For an autocrosser, shifting is not commonly a high-priority skill. In most autocross cars, the driver can put the car into second gear and drive the whole course without shifting again. More importantly, it's an advanced technique because it takes attention away from your primary job: keeping the car on line and under control.

When to Shift

Only shift when shifting will actually shave time on course. It has been said that one shift is the equivalent of three tenths of a second. When put that way, shifting should

enthusiasm. The only remedy at this point is to release the brakes and straighten the steering wheel (gently with both!) until the car responds.

The most important thing in autocross is to be able to be aggressive at corner exit. While you can shave a small amount of time by trail braking, you should never trail brake where it will reduce corner exit speeds or force you off line. Trail

braking should be regarded as a high-risk, low-reward activity. If trail braking into a particular corner is advantageous for some reason, be it an ill-handling car or a preferred line that demands it, so be it. For these reasons, it is worthwhile to add trail braking to your bag of tricks, but it should always be used sparingly, not as a basic skill.

While sometimes you do need to shift while on an autocross course, controlling your car is the first priority. In the flailing to get ready for this corner, the driver has turned on the windshield wipers (a rather common occurrence). Clearly, adding a downshift when approaching this corner would be an impossible task on this run. (Photo Courtesy Bryan Heitkotter)

Getting too greedy with the throttle at corner exit does not help run times. While it is important to be on the throttle early, well before the corner is finished, a driver needs to be very gentle with the throttle (especially in high-powered cars) in order to keep the car under control while exiting the corner. (Photo Courtesy Bryan Heitkotter)

be kept to a minimum. Drivers often shift at times when it just isn't necessary. The actual need to shift in a given situation varies greatly by car and driver.

A driver who has mastered upshifts and downshifts is able to shift more often without costing himself or herself time. Practice makes perfect. For drivers who are not quite as skilled, practicing gear changes should be done at events where results aren't as important. If the goal is the quickest possible time between the start and finish lights (and you have a limited number of attempts to get it right), it's not a good time for the unpracticed driver to try shifting.

A car with a wide torque band doesn't need to be downshifted as often as a car with a sharp power peak. This principle looks at what is to be gained by a downshift. For a car with a lot of torque, say a Corvette or Viper, a downshift may simply result in smoking the tires. For a car that is a slug when down in the revs, it can be critical to downshift.

The master shifters of autocross are the F125 drivers. These carts require shifting in order to be driven fast. Fortunately for these drivers, the shifter is just a flick of the wrist away. In production cars, shifting requires more planning and practice in order to execute a good shift every time. (Photo Courtesy Bryan Heitkotter)

Most autocross rides require taking a hand off the wheel to shift. This F125 driver has chosen a straight portion of the course to make the shift. Shifting in straights minimizes the chances for a mis-shift or loss of control. Not every shift can be conveniently located in a straight, however. (Photo Courtesy Bryan Heitkotter)

Some drivers don't have to shift at all. Formula 500 cars (F Modified) are an example of an autocross car that uses a snowmobile-type drivetrain. The engine is always kept near peak power and the transmission system continuously varies the gear ratio. (Photo Courtesy Bryan Heitkotter)

Some cars just aren't easy to downshift. While both the Subaru Impreza WRX and Honda S2000 suffer mightily when in low RPM, it is much more of a chore to downshift the Impreza into first gear. Thus, the Honda driver downshifts into first gear more often. In the risk-versus-reward discussion, the risk of missing the downshift in the Impreza outweighs the advantages of being in the lower gear.

When debating upshifting, consider how long the acceleration zone is after the shift. Hitting the rev limiter doesn't necessarily mean that you need to shift. The car will be slowing down while the clutch is depressed and the car is coasting. In order to make the upshift worthwhile, there needs to be some acceleration room after the shift. This is doubly true if the next corner is going to require a downshift!

It may not be advantageous to downshift when the car feels a little bogged down exiting a corner. When looking at downshifting, it is impor-

The Z06 Corvette is a dream for an autocrosser who hasn't mastered shifting. Lots of power and gobs of torque mean that most courses can be driven entirely in second gear. The split between cars that require regular shifting and those that don't is close to 50/50. (Photo Courtesy Bryan Heitkotter)

tant to consider how useful the extra torque will be. If you're already likely to have more power than you can use at corner exit, what advantage is there in downshifting? Similarly, if a downshift puts you into a gear that can only be used for half a second before being on the rev limiter in the lower gear, is the lower gear really helpful?

With all of that in mind, the decision of whether or not to attempt a shift needs to be made before leaving the starting line. In order to make the most of a shift, it needs to be placed carefully. Downshifts need to be made before acceleration starts. Upshifts need to be

made before the rev limiter is hit. Most importantly, make sure that you are going slow enough to not damage the engine when downshifting! When shifting is done in improv, minor mistakes will surely cost a few tenths here and there.

Heel-and-Toe Downshifting

The heel-and-toe downshifting technique is widely accepted to downshift while braking for a corner. This technique requires the driver to work the gas, brake, and clutch pedals all at the same time. Why use the gas pedal? It is important to match the engine's speed to the car's speed

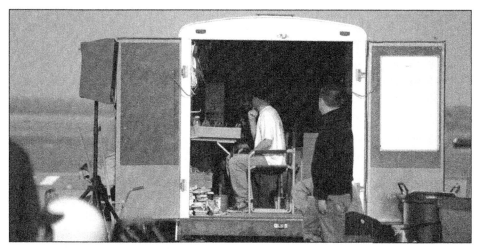

While the drivers and workers are doing their thing, timing and scoring keeps track of it all. There is a lot going on in the timing trailer and these workers don't need to be interrupted. If there is a problem with timing and scoring, take it to another event official to get it sorted out. (Photo Courtesy Bryan Heitkotter)

Cars with narrow torque bands, such as the Honda S2000 and Lotus Elise, are liable to make a driver row the gears. Drivers in these cars need to master downshifting and upshifting in order to turn fast times. (Photo Courtesy Bryan Heitkotter)

When performing a heel-and-toe downshift, the right foot operates both the brake pedal and the throttle. If it is difficult to accomplish this feat in your car, consider altering the pedals (if legal) or changing shoes. The goal is to have the brake firmly depressed while the throttle is just blipped.

when downshifting. This requires the driver to rev the engine. Failing to do so will upset the car.

Selecting a lower gear forces the engine to speed up. When downshifting from a gear with a net ratio of 9:1 to one with a net ratio of 12:1, the engine speeds up by the ratio of 12:9. That is to say that an engine turning 3,600 rpm before the downshift will be turning 4,800 rpm after the downshift. Even though you're braking, you're not going to scrub 25 percent of your speed during the

downshift. One way or another, the engine is going to speed up.

There are two ways the engine can speed up. The first is by using what is called engine braking. This means that the car's momentum and energy is used to speed up the engine. This is an effective way to slow the car, but it applies a very harsh braking force to the drive wheels, often causing them to slip. The other way to speed the engine up is using the throttle to rev it up while the clutch is depressed. This

eliminates any engine braking, but it also doesn't add any demand to the drive wheels.

So, in order to keep from upsetting the car, you need to run all three pedals during a downshift. Failure to do so has the same effect of accelerating with too much vigor.

Heel-and-toe downshifting is an interesting dance on the pedals. The left foot works the clutch pedal while the right foot manages both the brake and the throttle. While the purpose of this technique is to select a lower gear, you must not forget that braking must be your primary function. Fail to brake enough (or brake too much), and basic car control is compromised.

To ensure adequate control of the brake pedal, place the ball and big toe of your right foot firmly on the brake. When braking, depress the clutch pedal and select the lower

Downshifting: Slipping it in Late

Having trouble mastering the heel-toe maneuver? You're not alone. It takes considerable coordination to downshift while operating three pedals simultaneously. Those who haven't mastered the fancy footwork resort to a downshifting method that is sometimes referred to as "slipping it in late."

Slipping it in late involves downshifting after braking is finished. There is a compromise with this technique. Perhaps several. The compromises cost a little time on course as compared to an accomplished heel-toe downshifter. For the driver lacking in footwork, there are few reasonable alternatives.

The basic premise to this technique is that there will be some time in the early-middle of the corner when the car is just rolling. The driver needs to be off the brakes, but isn't ready to accelerate yet. In this half second of time, the driver can downshift without needing to run all three pedals and without losing time under acceleration.

The sequence is this:
- Brake for the corner
- Roll off of brakes and turn in to corner
- Depress clutch and move gear selector to lower gear
- Rev engine to match engine RPM to vehicle speed
- Release clutch
- Start unwinding wheel and accelerate

The compromises are that some control of the steering wheel must be surrendered (the right hand is off the wheel mid-corner) and acceleration may be delayed somewhat. This technique isn't the best in the world, but it works. The time lost is not often significant. At the very least, the technique keeps you on course while learning the heel-toe technique.

At the entrance of the corner, there is a time when the driver is off the brakes but isn't yet ready to accelerate. For those who haven't mastered the heel-and-toe downshifting technique, this is the right time to downshift. When done properly, the shift is complete just before the car reaches the apex. (Photo Courtesy Bryan Heitkotter)

After reaching the apex, the downshift must be complete. By this point in the corner, the driver should be worrying about accelerating out of the corner rather than making sure the car is in the correct gear. (Photo Courtesy Bryan Heitkotter)

gear. When preparing to release the clutch, use the right side or heel of the foot (depending on personal preference and pedal layout) to give the throttle a quick blip. During this part of the operation, maintain steady pressure on the brake pedal. With the engine RPM up, the clutch pedal can be safely released.

Easy to say, hard to perfect. The important thing to remember is that braking is the top priority. When revving the engine, you only need to be close to the right engine speed. It's better to rev the engine too high than not high enough. As with all other driving habits, this should be practiced on the street before it is attempted on the autocross course.

Left-Foot Braking

We were all taught in driver's education that our left foot wasn't

Autocross, by its nature, is a family sport. With most clubs having Ladies classes, a family can work out a system where both parents can participate and be able to watch the kids. Many parents with teenagers use autocross to teach car control.

Left-foot brakers are given away by their brake lights. When a car has brake lights illuminated in a section that should be nearly full throttle, a left-foot braker is at the wheel. One drawback of left-foot braking is unconsciously resting the left foot on the brake pedal. This drags the brakes lightly and can cost small bits of time. (Photo Courtesy Bryan Heitkotter)

Cars in Prepared and Modified classes have significantly more room for modification than cars in Stock classes. Drivers in these cars can easily tailor the cockpit to match their specific needs. This luxury makes tasks like fancy footwork much easier to accomplish. (Photo Courtesy Bryan Heitkotter)

supposed to be used on the brake pedal. If we use our left foot for braking, we'll be prone to resting it on the pedal and dragging the brakes all the time. This hurts fuel economy and wears brakes out quickly. And our brake lights are on all the time—no one knows when we are really braking. Danger, danger! While there is some truth to that, a lot of the concern doesn't apply to autocrossing. Actually, left-foot braking can save time and improve car control.

Using your right foot on both the accelerator and brake pedals works. If it didn't, they wouldn't teach you this when you learn to drive. But, with one foot pulling double duty, you're always moving your foot back and forth between the pedals. Left-foot braking is a way to shorten the time that it takes to transition from the accelerator to the brake and back again. Contrary to what is commonly said, there are

few advantages to using both the throttle and the brake at the same time. That's not why you want to left-foot brake.

The advantages of left-foot braking are pretty obvious. While the general idea is to brake, turn, and accelerate in that order (which doesn't inherently favor either right-foot or left-foot brakers), sometimes you have to adjust what you're doing. A driver using his right foot to operate both pedals has a very brief delay between acceleration and braking. A driver using his left foot to operate

the brake pedal can apply the brakes almost instantly upon recognizing the need. When you make a mistake and you start into recovery, the left-foot braker has the advantage of quicker response. This advantage translates into less time lost and a quicker run.

Why don't you want to left-foot brake? Left-foot braking is, like any skill, one that has to be learned and perfected. While you've spent your whole life right-foot braking, your left foot spends its time resting and pressing the clutch. If you don't practice it, you are better off right-foot braking. Additionally, when you're left-foot braking and need to shift, you have to dance your feet around. If this hasn't been practiced extensively, it will go badly.

Be prepared for some mis-steps when practicing. It is common for a beginning left-foot braker to be thrown into the steering wheel after pressing the brake pedal like the clutch. It's also reasonably common to press the brake pedal instead of the clutch, which is especially embarrassing under acceleration. Most importantly, don't feel like you *need* to left-foot brake. Some very fast drivers use their right foot to brake.

So, if you intend to left-foot brake, make sure you practice. This will enhance pedal feel of the left foot (it wants to go straight to the floor, remember?) and help you get used to moving the left foot around. This practice will help make sure that you press the brake pedal when you want brakes and press the clutch pedal when you want to shift. It's tough to council someone to practice a technique like this on the street, but that's where it should be tried. Preferably alone, where nobody can see what happens.

Launching

Launching isn't an advanced topic because it's difficult. It's an advanced topic because it isn't necessary to autocross successfully on most courses. Drag racers know that trimming a tenth or two off of their 60-foot times leads to significant gains in elapsed time. This isn't true in autocross.

Autocross courses aren't set up to emphasize the launch. Actually, courses are typically set up to minimize the need for a good launch. ProSolo events excepted, launching

Footwear

A driver's shoes can be nearly as important as the feet in them. Anyone who has driven in OSHA-approved work boots can tell you that it is a lot harder than driving in tennis shoes. Attempting a heel-toe downshift in work boots would be laughable.

Look for shoes that are flexible, both in the sole and the upper. This flexibility affords you a greater level of feel. This feel is important for key items like throttle modulation and threshold braking. A flexible shoe is also nearly imperative for such techniques as left-foot braking and heel-toe downshifting.

There are a wide variety of options out there. Aqua socks and boating "deck shoes" are very popular among drivers because of their minimal material. Many drivers who use common athletic shoes are at the top of their class. Several shoe companies have started making "designer" race shoes (these look like race shoes, but don't carry the SFI fire-resistant certifications) that look to be decent choices. Another choice is a true SFI-certified racing shoe like road racers wear. These shoes are made for driving, but tend to carry a higher price tag.

Whatever shoes you choose, keep the intended use in mind. Some cars have very tight pedal spacing. In this case, a tight-fitting shoe is helpful to keep the feet only where they're intended to be. Sometimes the pedals are spaced farther apart and a wide shoe is helpful for heel-toe downshifting. If the shoes are likely to be used for course walking, comfort should be a priority.

When it comes to footwear, autocrossers have a lot of choices. The only restriction is that the shoe must cover the entire foot (the sandal in the back isn't acceptable). While street shoes are OK, more flexible shoes are popular. The shoe on the left is a true racing shoe, while the black and red shoe is a type of water sock. Both are excellent choices.

hard at the start of an autocross course is usually a good way to cost yourself time. Many courses have tight corners built into the start, and being off line at the exit of these corners usually adds more time than the perfect launch might shave.

When launching is helpful, you want to make the most of it. This means putting power down effectively

Making a good, clean start is the foundation of a great autocross run. Some courses give a driver room to launch the car hard, but most courses have a tight corner right off the starting line. When this is the case, the best policy is to safely negotiate the corner and then worry about going fast. (Photo Courtesy Bryan Heitkotter)

Getting aggressive at the start of a course isn't always a good idea. With a lot of horsepower and first gear, it is easy to upset the car at the start. Once the car is off line or sideways, you spend time trying to recover. The run is barely started and you're already behind. (Photo Courtesy Bryan Heitkotter)

On a course that allows for a serious launch (like a ProSolo), all-wheel-drive cars have an advantage over their two-wheel-drive counterparts. The advantage can be substantial—often half a second in the first 60 feet. (Photo Courtesy Bryan Heitkotter)

start. If the engine speed is too low, the engine will bog and the start will be just plain sluggish. It takes practice to get this right.

In all-wheel-drive cars, the launch is much simpler. These cars, with the exception of STU and SM cars, don't typically have enough power to generate significant wheelspin. This means there's very little technique involved. The battle here is to keep the engine from bogging without smoking the clutch or breaking drivetrain components. Many all-wheel-drive cars have broken at the starting line (transmission and axles, mostly) and many more have had clutches with very short service lives. Even considering all of that, the rewards for launching an all-wheel-drive car are immense. All-wheel-drive cars can gain up to half a second on their two-wheel-drive competition before the 60-foot mark when launched properly!

Regardless of the car, launching is hard on parts. This is a bigger concern for some cars than for others. Given the limited usefulness of the launch on the typical autocross course, a driver can gain more time focusing on and practicing other skills.

without bogging the engine. Spinning the tires doesn't help a car accelerate. This is comparable to locking the brakes, and it actually hurts acceleration (just as a locked wheel hurts braking). Unfortunately, the car can't accelerate to 30 mph instantly. Without any wheelspin, either the engine will bog or the clutch must be slipped (usually burning it to a crisp). It can be a delicate situation.

In two-wheel-drive cars, the launch is typically a balance between too much and too little wheelspin. These cars usually have enough power to spin the tires and then some. The trick is releasing the clutch with the engine speed just high enough to spin the tires a little bit. If the engine speed is too high, wheelspin will be excessive and the result is a sluggish, tire-smoking

ProSolo Starts

Unlike normal drag racing, ProSolo runs are made in short succession. A pair of cars is started about every 30 seconds. The cars on course may not even be finished before the next pair is started. This leads to a fast-paced event with a lot of action.

When the light turns green, it is time to go. With the bracket-racing format of the Challenge Rounds of a ProSolo event, the cars are started at different times. The first car back to the finish line has the advantage of a lead going into second runs of the matchup. The cars then swap courses and do it again. The winner of the round is determined by the margins of victory of the two matches. (Photo Courtesy Bryan Heitkotter)

The side-by-side action is what makes ProSolo different from all other forms of autocross. Spectators can see who is ahead as the cars make their way through the course. There is also usually a place on the course where drivers can see the other car and know whether they are winning or losing the duel.

ProSolo is the one type of autocross event that really emphasizes the start. These events use a sportsman-style drag-racing "Christmas tree" to start the runs. Reaction time counts and the start is commonly straight for around 200 feet. Combining all of this with typically short courses (30 to 40 seconds), the start is significant.

Two things govern the start of a ProSolo run: the electronic eyes at the starting line and the starting lights. In order for a car to start a ProSolo run without a foul, two things must happen. The car must be in the staging beam when the tree starts and the car must not break the start beam before the lights turn green and the timer starts. There's nothing fancy about this; drag racers have done it for decades. In fact, the local drag strip is a great place to practice starts.

In the autocross world, there are really only two things to complicate the start. Autocross sites aren't always level. Sometimes cars have weird appendages (like tow hooks) that make

staging and starting difficult. Both of these problems are easily overcome.

When a ProSolo event has the start placed in a location that isn't level, sometimes the car wants to roll. In a perfect world you stage the car and release the brake, clutch depressed, and wait for the tree. If the car wants to roll, you might roll out of the staging light and have your run disqualified. ProSolo events typically have ample time to stage so the problem can be realized early in the staging process. If it happens, the hand brake can be used to hold the car in place. In this situation, the hand brake is released as the driver launches the car. To make this easier, the rules allow the locking mechanism on the hand brake to be disabled for ProSolo events. The easiest way to do this is to tape the button down with some sturdy duct tape.

Occasionally, cars have something low at the front that isn't substantial enough to use for reliable staging but does break the start beam. An example would be the front valence on a C5 Corvette or other air dam. When this happens, it is often very difficult to get consistent and clean starts. Additionally, drivers with this problem are at a serious disadvantage as they are effectively deep staged in an extreme way. This reduces the driver's speed at the starting lights and adds elapsed time to the run. So, the rules permit a competitor to add material at the front of the car to facilitate staging. This commonly shows itself as a piece of cardboard taped below the front air dam. This cardboard extends from the air dam back to the leading edge of the front tires. This assures the driver that he or she is staging with the same part of the car that breaks the start beam.

Most front-wheel-drive cars have more than enough power to spin the tires at the start. Cars without limited-slip differentials are especially prone to wheelspin. Launching these cars requires patience and feel, as smoking the tires isn't much faster than bogging the engine. (Photo Courtesy Bryan Heitkotter)

The Advantages of Being Early

This isn't really a technique, so much as an opportunity to extol the virtues of being early. It can't be said enough. Staying ahead of the car and the course is key to being fast. This comes in two parts; one that is proactive and one that is semi-reactive.

A driver who stays ahead of the course is always in a position to be aggressive. This much is obvious. More importantly, a driver who stays ahead of the course has options when a mistake is made. Braking early to set up for a late apex line affords a driver some recovery room if the corner is misjudged. Keeping ahead of a slalom gives some margin for any needed steering corrections. If you are looking three to five seconds ahead, as suggested in Chapter 2, you'll be looking about three slalom cones ahead.

A driver who is anticipating the car's response to inputs will react more quickly to slips and errors. Being ahead of the car in this manner allows a driver to be a little more aggressive. The car's response is expected and the driver's next input is automatic. A quicker reaction leads to more precise car control and less time lost due to small driver errors.

Being early on the course is what allows a driver to be aggressive. Being just a few feet late when braking or turning in for an element can cause serious problems. This driver missed the apex by about 3 feet. This is going to cause a loss of several tenths of a second. (Photo Courtesy Bryan Heitkotter)

This driver is much closer to the apex. While the driver of the Trans-Am is still trying to negotiate the first part of this element, this driver is looking toward the exit of the element. In a few more feet, this driver can apply throttle and accelerate away. (Photo Courtesy Bryan Heitkotter)

STOCK CATEGORY: CAR PREPARATION AND TUNING

Stock category is considered to be a driver's class. The car's modifications from the production car are very limited and often classes are populated with many examples of the same model. A Stock enjoys a strong following from Honda S2000 owners. (Photo Courtesy Bryan Heitkotter)

The Stock classes are intended to be filled with commonly available and popular sports cars and sporty sedans. The Corvette is an excellent example of meeting this intent. The C4 Corvette is still competitive in A Stock. Expensive and hard-to-find cars are often excluded from the Stock category to encourage participation. (Photo Courtesy Bryan Heitkotter)

What's Allowed

The formula for SCCA's Stock category is simple. The car must compete as specified by the manufacturer with few exceptions. Winners separate themselves from the rest by how they use the few legal preparation allowances and how well they drive.

Cars are divided into nine different classes based on their performance potential on an autocross course. The rules generally don't allow competitors to radically change the way the car behaves. In other words, the heart and soul of the Stock-category autocross car is essentially the same as it was when it rolled off the assembly line. Most of preparing a car for competition in a Stock class is dealing with the car's weaknesses.

The description of cars allowed in Stock category is pretty broad. Generally speaking, any car that was mass produced for the United States domestic market and available for purchase through the normal dealer system is legal in its appropriate Stock class. The rulebook has an extensive list of cars in each class. Cars that aren't listed need to be produced in quantities of more than

The Toyota MR-2 is a popular car in E Stock. Over the years, there has been much debate about which exact variant of the car is the most competitive. Serious competitors have gravitated toward cars without sunroofs or T-tops and with features like ABS. At the local level, a driver can win in any variant of the car. (Photo Courtesy Bryan Heitkotter)

1,000 in a model year to be eligible. Cars that are specifically listed in the "exclusion" list are, obviously, ineligible for Stock classes.

The list of legal modifications in Stock category is very short. The generic list of major items is below:

- Exhaust system downstream of the last catalytic converter may be modified or replaced.
- Any wheel of the same diameter and width as stock with an offset within 1/4 inch of stock may be used.
- Any DOT-legal tire meeting the SCCA requirements and fitting on a legal wheel may be used.
- Any damper or shock absorber with two or fewer external adjustments that retains that stock suspension geometry may be used.
- Any front sway bar may be used.
- Normally expendable items (air filter, oil filter, spark plugs, brake pads, etc.) may be replaced with non-factory units.

In addition to that list of modifications, Stock-class cars can use any adjustment methods authorized for non-competition use by the factory (either by Technical Service Bulletins or Factory Service Manual). This means that the alignment can be adjusted. Cars with active suspension systems or traction control can configure the system in any factory authorized way.

Often a model of car was available from the factory in several different model years, option packages, or trim levels. The SCCA specifies that a competitor may not mix specifications from different model years, option packages, or trim levels. The rules also indicate that a competitor may convert a car to a different option package or trim level provided the conversion is complete and the car could have been delivered from the factory in this alternate configuration.

The rules do not allow dealer-installed options to be legal in Stock category. The line gets a little blurry when looking at imports, however. The SCCA has allowed some port-installed options to be legal by ruling that the port facility in North America is an extension of the factory. This decision is based on the fact that some automakers use the port as the point of final assembly for certain components in popular option packages.

Evaluating the "Stock" Automobile

The very first step to preparing any car is evaluating it. If you've driven the car any amount, you've got a good idea about how the car will

The Mazda Miata has been another mainstay of the Stock classes. Currently, the cars are legal in both C Stock (1999+ models) and E Stock (1990–1997 models.) In years past, the Solo National Championships saw grids of 40 or more Miatas in a single class. (Photo Courtesy Bryan Heitkotter)

Selecting a Car for Stock Category

This topic is for both the driver who wants to transition into being the serious autocrosser with an eye on National-level competition, and the casual driver who is looking to buy a new car and wants it to be competitive. It's obvious that there are lots of cars out there and not very many classes. So, some cars are going to be more competitive than others. Here's a quick rundown of the types of cars found in each class:

Superstock: Ultra high-performance sports cars

A Stock: High-performance sports cars and sport sedans

B Stock: Moderate- and high-performance sports cars

C Stock: Low- and moderate-performance sports cars

D Stock: Moderate-performance sport sedans

E Stock: Low-performance budget sports cars

F Stock: High-performance large sedans

G Stock: Moderate-performance small sedans

H Stock: Low-performance sedans

Super Stock is the home of the high-performance sports car. Cars like the Lotus Elise, Z06 Corvette, and Porsche 911 GT3 consistently reside at the top of the results lists. A driver doesn't need one of these cars to play in Super Stock, but should expect to see them in the class. (Photo Courtesy Bryan Heitkotter)

B Stock is home to quite a few sports cars. While the Mazda RX-8 and Nissan 350Z are the current top dogs in the class, older cars like the Toyota MR-2 Turbo are still competitive on the local level. For those just out to have fun, gems like the Jaguar XKE are also classed here. (Photo Courtesy Bryan Heitkotter)

D Stock is the residence of the sporty sedan. This Subaru WRX competes there, along with the BMW 3-series sedans (non-M) and the Lexus IS-series sedans. The autocross performance of these cars is lower than the true sports car, but these are still fun to drive. (Photo Courtesy Bryan Heitkotter)

For those who need to be having fun in an economical but fun-to-drive car, H Stock is probably the category to be. The top cars in this class include the Mini Cooper and the Honda Civic Si. There are lots of fun cars in this class and the possibilities are nearly endless. (Photo Courtesy Bryan Heitkotter)

Perusing the latest results from National Solo events is a good way to see what's currently on top within a particular class. Magazine articles are good references, but road and track testing is so far from the needs of the autocrosser that you won't get much out of the article other than an impression of what the car is like. A couple good clues to the perfor-mance of a car are the curb weight and size of the tires. Low weight and wide tires are a good indicator that the car is intended for performance.

In general, non-performance-related options are frowned upon. These typically add weight and reduce performance. Similarly, sun-roofs and convertible variants are sel-dom as competitive as hardtop models. On the other hand, drivetrain and suspension options are typically good buys. If a limited-slip differential is an available option, take it. Wider wheels? They're an advantage, too.

Just remember: When customiz-ing a new purchase, the only legal options are factory options. Dealer-installed items are not legal in the Stock category.

With a limited number of Stock classes and only a handful of cars that are popular in each class, "clones" are rather common. These Toyota MR-2s compete against each other in E Stock. Without car numbers, it would be difficult for course workers to tell them apart. (Photo Courtesy Bryan Heitkotter)

When selecting a car to buy based on autocross performance, specific option packages need to be considered. The Corvette is a top car in Super Stock, but the road to the winner's circle it tough if you aren't driving a Z06 model Corvette. Other models of car have similar variations that are preferred by autocrossers. (Photo Courtesy Bryan Heitkotter)

There is a stock class for just about every car. H Stock is a common location for the non-sporty cars that people want to autocross. These cars need a little extra attention during car setup to perform well on the course, as they weren't intended to be driven at the limit. (Photo Courtesy Bryan Heitkotter)

The first step to making a Stock class car faster is figuring out its strengths and weaknesses. If a competitor can identify what parts of the car need to be improved in order to go faster, it is much easier to get the most out of the car. (Photo Courtesy Bryan Heitkotter)

With wheel size restricted, competitors are squeezed into a few options. Some cars have few options, possibly being restricted to the stock wheels. Other cars, such as the Mazda RX-8, use a relatively common size wheel.

behave. Knowing this behavior is a good place to start.

The average production automobile has two common traits. Most cars are delivered from the factory with a healthy dose of understeer built into them and most cars have difficulty harnessing their full power in anything other than a straight line. Bad news: These problems are usually hard to fix within the Stock category rules, and the addition of sticky, R-compound tires generally makes the problems worse. Several of the common conventions for tuning cars are thrown out the window when fighting to make a car well behaved within the confines of the Stock category rules.

Tires and Wheels

As mentioned earlier, tires are critical to a competitive performance.

R-compound tires are legal in the SCCA's Stock category. For those who can't make that kind of a commitment, many clubs offer an indexed Street Tire class. These classes allow competitors to have fun and compete on a relatively level playing field without the need for extra wheels and race tires. (Photo Courtesy Bryan Heitkotter)

A torque wrench is an autocrosser's best friend, or at least one of them. With tire changes at the event being common, an autocrosser needs to have an accurately calibrated torque wrench to make sure everything is tightened properly. (Photo Courtesy Bryan Heitkotter)

Wheels are restricted to a specified size. As you might expect, there are a few secrets here.

At regional events, you can sometimes be competitive with a high-performance street tire. Generally speaking, the competitive Stock class driver will have a second set of stock (sized) wheels with a set of R-compound tires mounted on them. Given the nature of R-compound tires, this usually means changing tires at an event or towing the car to and from events. Often, changing tires at an event requires towing a tire trailer behind the car. This is a level of commitment that some autocrossers can't afford to make. If this is you, look to a regional Street Tire class for competition.

Under no circumstances should a serious competitor expect to get a whole autocross season out of one set of R-compound tires. Here's why: first, the tires wear very quickly; second, even if there is plenty of rubber left on a tire, tires simply get hard from age and use and don't grip the pavement as well as when new. The general consensus is that R-compound tires have the most grip during their first 30 runs. On some cars, the tires may wear out faster than that, showing cords in as few as 15 runs. On other cars, the tires may last for hundreds of runs after they quit being sticky. If tire wear is a problem, rotate the tires at every event.

For those who can make the commitment to run R-compound tires, there are two decisions: Which brand to buy, and what size? This might seem like two independent questions, but they're not. With R-compound tires being limited in size availability, sometimes a size preference can dictate brand choice, and vice versa.

The Acura Integra Type R is an incredible performer in D Stock. One of the quirks of this car is the narrow wheels. Look at the front tires. That's a 225-series tire, a full 9 inches wide, crammed onto a 6-inch-wide wheel. Wider tires have proven to be faster, even though they are pinched on the wheels. (Photo Courtesy Bryan Heitkotter)

This Hoosier tire is an excellent example of an R-compound tire. There is no real tread, just two circumferential grooves. The tire, while DOT legal, is not recommended for highway use. In a nutshell, this tire was built for only one purpose—racing. Hoosier takes this one step further; they build tires specifically for autocrossers. (Photo Courtesy Bryan Heitkotter)

There are three things to consider when choosing a tire size: overall diameter, width, and load capacity. The typical way to make this decision is to look at tires in that order. After trimming the choices to the tires that fit on the stock wheels for your car, eliminate sizes that are clearly too tall or too short for your application (remember that tire diameter affects gearing!). Now you're down to probably two choices in each brand of tire. Pick the widest tire that fits on your car without rubbing the fenders or other parts of the chassis. Then, check the load capacity of the tire to make sure it will carry your car (it probably will). The last step is to check to make sure that this tire will actually mount onto your stock wheels. Sometimes it's dif-

This Hoosier tire is worn out. Hoosiers are well known for a short life expectancy on cars without adequate negative camber. The tires are very fast for a few runs. On cars that can achieve enough negative camber, Hoosier tires last a long time. (Photo Courtesy Bryan Heitkotter)

ficult to mount a 9-inch-wide tire onto a 6-inch-wide wheel.

Since 2000, Hoosier and Kumho have been the two most popular manufacturers of R-compound tires. In 2007, Hankook showed its latest products are capable of being competitive as well.

Hoosier Tires

A brief history of the R-compound market would show that Hoosier has changed its autocross-specific R-compound tire (the A-series tire) nearly every year. Every change has been a step toward higher performance. Hoosier's reputation has been that its tire is likely the best choice on the surface where the SCCA Solo National Championships are held and it's no worse than second best on any other surface.

Another important observation about Hoosier's autocross tires is that they are not long lasting. The latest tires are known for wearing out very quickly on cars that can't get enough negative camber (a common Stock class problem) and sometimes don't last through 20 competitive runs before showing cords. The other historical problem for Hoosier tires has been what is referred to as "heat-cycling out," where the tire still has plenty of tread but has lost its grip from lots of use. While all of the R-compound tires heat-cycle out, Hoosier tires have been known to suffer this after fewer runs than other brands.

Hoosier also produces a rain tire that has shown itself to be the best wet-weather DOT tire in autocross by a large margin. From 2004 to 2007, the choices in the rain were the Hoosier Radial Wet or being non-competitive. Other tires have won big events in the rain, but the consensus is that driver talent is largely responsible for those results.

Because race tires are Hoosier's only product line, the tires are priced accordingly, being on the expensive end of the scale. Many of the top drivers run Hoosiers for their performance. Many are also rewarded with free tires from Hoosier for winning big events. It's a marketing cycle that keeps Hoosier at the top of the results sheet and keeps competitive buyers opening their wallets for what appears to be the fastest tire out there.

Kumho Tires

Kumho is much less aggressive in the race tire market. Race tires are a very small part of Kumho's business and, to be honest, the product reflects that. However, Kumho produces a high-quality tire that is very competitive with (and sometimes superior to) Hoosier's offerings.

The Hoosier Radial Wet has been the only choice for autocrossers in the rain. This tire has consistently proven itself to be the fastest DOT tire in the rain. The tires are spendy and can't be used on dry pavement, but for those intent on winning it is the only choice. (Photo Courtesy Bryan Heitkotter)

Hoosier, like other tire manufacturers, rewards winning drivers with prizes. These prizes are paid to winners at National Tour, ProSolo, and National Championship events. There are two requirements to win: The car must have Hoosier tires on all four corners and the car must have Hoosier decals in the prescribed locations. (Photo Courtesy Bryan Heitkotter)

Unfortunately, Kumho is much slower to react to changes in technology and the market and seems to introduce a new tire every three years or so. At many sites, the Kumho V710 is the equal of Hoosier's latest offering, and the next tire produced by Kumho will likely give similar results.

Kumho's race tires (the V710 and the Victoracer that came before it) last longer than the Hoosier A-series tires. While the heat-cycling problems are similar, very few drivers have reported cording a V710 in less than 30 runs, even on camber-challenged cars. Drivers in cars that are easy on tires can expect the V710 to heat-cycle out and last well over 100 runs before seeing cords.

Drivers on Kumhos have always been at a disadvantage in the rain. The historic choices have been to run Kumho's top wet-weather street tire or the V710. Both tires are noticeably slower than the Hoosier Radial Wets in the rain. Kumho is expected to introduce a rain-specific R-compound tire to battle with the Hoosier. As the tire hasn't yet been tested in competition, it is unknown how competitive the tire will be. Expectations are high.

Kumho tires have historically been less expensive than Hoosier's offerings. With recent increases in fuel costs and a weakening U.S. dollar, the Kumho tires (produced in Korea) have been priced about the same as Hoosiers. Many top drivers have won on the V710 and its predecessor, the Victoracer. While the tires appear to be a tick slower than the Hoosier, the V710 has shown that it can win on any given day.

Hankook Tires

The information about the Hankook tire is pretty limited. The latest DOT-legal R-compound offering from Hankook has shown to be competitive with Kumho and Hoosier, but it hasn't won anything major yet. That may simply be the result of many top drivers not being willing to take a chance on the "new kid on

Kumho tires are a perennial winner at autocross events around the country. Historically, Kumho tires have been less expensive than their Hoosier counterparts but have not been quite as quick. The advantage of the Kumho has been longevity. Everyone seems to get a lot of runs out of the Kumho tires. (Photo Courtesy Bryan Heitkotter)

Wheel Health

Autocross causes very high stresses on wheels. It makes sense. The wheel transfers the tire's force to the chassis. At the same time, you're trying to reduce weight in your car as much as possible. Lightweight wheels and high stresses can be a bad combination.

The first rule of wheels is that three qualities are desirable: light, strong, and cheap. But you can only have two of the three. In reality, there are only two choices to make: light and strong (but expensive!) or strong and cheap (and heavy!). An autocross wheel that isn't strong is not worth having around.

After choosing a set of wheels and having the best tires money can buy mounted on them, there is still some work to do. You might think that the first autocross will test the strength of the wheels, and that a successful event means a good wheel choice. While this might be true, there's still one problem to consider. This problem usually rears its ugly head after you've been using the wheels for a while.

The stresses of autocross can crack the spokes of wheels through metal fatigue. Metals, by their nature, are susceptible to cracking due to cyclical loading. Cracks form due to repeated application of high stresses. Sounds like autocross. Because of this, it is important to periodically inspect wheels for cracks.

A fatigue crack starts very small and grows over time. A visual inspection often catches fatigue cracks before the wheel fails completely. To get the most out of an inspection, thoroughly clean the wheels and let them dry. Use a high-intensity light and look at the wheels from several angles. The better the inspection, the more likely you are to find a crack while it's still small!.

If you uncover something worrisome, there are places that can perform more thorough inspection of the wheel using non-destructive methods. A local high-performance engine shop often has the equipment on hand to do the testing, or know someone who can.

In the quest to find lightweight wheels, this driver has mixed and matched. The front wheels are from a Mazda Millenia while the rear wheels are an aftermarket design. Both wheels are very light and should be checked for cracks regularly. (Photo Courtesy Bryan Heitkotter)

The owner of this Mazda RX-8 purchased a set of OZ Racing Ultraleggeras. These wheels shaved a few pounds off the weight of the stock wheels. If you are going to buy a second set of wheels for autocross, finding a lightweight set makes sense. (Photo Courtesy Bryan Heitkotter)

the block." It's clear that the Hankook tire is not vastly superior to the Kumho and Hoosier tires, but it's not clear yet whether or not the tire is inferior either.

The Hankook tire seems to be on par with the Kumho for durability. With limited data available, the jury is still out regarding how much longevity the tire really has. Hankook does seem to be making an attempt to catch up for lost time in the R&D department. With luck it means that there will soon be a well-recognized and reliable third choice in the tire game.

Pricing of Hankook tires is appealing. Hankook seems to be trying to tap the market of folks who want an inexpensive but competitive tire. It seems to be working, as they

At a regional autocross event, tire selection is often made on the basis of what is available and economical. It is not common for a regional autocross champion to spend a lot of money putting the best tires on their car for every event. (Photo Courtesy Bryan Heitkotter)

Kumho tires are a perennial winner at autocross events around the country. Historically, Kumho tires have been less expensive than their Hoosier counterparts, but have not been quite as quick. The advantage of the Kumho has been longevity. Everyone seems to get a lot of runs out of the Kumho tires. (Photo Courtesy Bryan Heitkotter)

are slowly gaining a foothold in the market, particularly in the tire sizes that Kumho doesn't produce.

Wheels

What about wheels? They have to be stock size. This means the same diameter, width, and offset as the stock wheel. Well, the offset can vary from stock by 1/4 inch or less. The size restriction often means that there are few legal wheel choices.

The preferred wheels in Stock class are always the lightest wheels that are legal. Every pound matters and wheel weight counts more than most other weight—this weight is also rotating and is unsprung. A couple pounds per wheel will be noticed on most cars, particularly small and low-powered ones. Of course, this usually comes with a steep price tag.

Those who autocross popular cars have strength in numbers. There are lots of other competitors to help you find the lightest or most economical wheels. Popular cars also tend to have more wheel choices being manufactured for them. If you're in this boat, the question is: How much do you want to spend?

Some research needs to be done for those in less popular cars. If there are no good choices other than stock, two avenues present themselves: Be satisfied with the stock wheels or spend a large sum of money on a set of custom wheels. Companies that produce race wheels can make wheels to a specification for a price. These wheels, in addition to being expensive and requiring a relatively long time from order to delivery, are often lighter than their off-the-shelf counterparts. For those going this route, don't be surprised to spend significantly more than $2,000 for a set of wheels.

The Front Sway Bar

Choosing a proper front sway bar for a Stock category car has been the subject of extensive testing and experimentation over the years. There's a simple reason: The front sway bar is the only tool available in the Stock classes to reduce body roll or alter the relative roll stiffness of the car.

The staggered wheel width on the Honda S2000 makes finding wheels difficult. Mixing wheels from different sources is a necessity. The staggered width also means that a driver can't rotate tires from front to back. Fortunately, the car is relatively easy on tires. (Photo Courtesy Bryan Heitkotter)

Fuel Load

Running low on fuel would seem to be a good way to reduce the weight of a car. With gasoline weighing a little over 6 pounds per gallon, a car with a large tank has a lot of "extra" fuel sloshing around. Before you run it dry before an event, consider this: Running with a lot of fuel in the tank might be helpful.

The high g-loading that is experienced on the autocross course doesn't just pull you around in your seat. It also pulls the fuel around in the tank. The intake for the fuel pump might be at the bottom of the tank, but what if the fuel isn't? Sputter, cough. This is called fuel starvation.

Fuel starvation is actually pretty common. Every car will starve for fuel at some point; the question is when. The trend is for sports cars to have fuel systems designed for high-g cornering. Sedans tend to starve for fuel more easily, due to less design thought being given to sporty

driving. The problem is most common at the exit of long corners. Here, the engine can empty the fuel line between the fuel pump located in the gas tank and the fuel pump at the engine. Once this supply is gone, the car sputters.

Regardless of what you drive, the only way to know how low you can go is to test it. Every car is different, even examples of the same model of car. A car can even starve more easily when turning one direction rather than the other. Some Subaru Imprezas need more than half a tank of fuel to keep from starving on long right-hand corners. Some Mazda Miatas can run on fumes and turn hard either way.

The 25 pounds that is saved by running a low fuel load isn't worth the time lost if you suffer from starvation. At big events, make sure you've got enough fuel. At practice days or "fun" events, test to see how low your car can go.

How much fuel is in your tank? Weight does matter to an autocrosser, but excess fuel may not be a bad thing. Stock category cars can't improve the fuel system to make sure they can get all of the gasoline out of the tank while on course. Some models of car suffer from fuel starvation, or temporarily running out of fuel due to cornering forces. (Photo Courtesy Bryan Heitkotter)

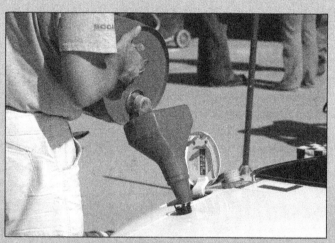

Adding a little fuel to the tank can stop fuel starvation. If you know this can be a problem, bringing fuel to the event isn't a bad idea. Refueling should be done with a fire extinguisher handy, however. Refueling a hot racecar isn't exactly the safest thing to do. (Photo Courtesy Bryan Heitkotter)

For many common autocross cars—those that tend to understeer with inadequate front camber—the front sway bar is a two-way street. On one hand, theory says that a softer front sway bar will help the front tires work more efficiently by letting the rear tires do more work. On the other hand, theory also says that a stiffer front sway bar (reducing total body roll) will help tires work more efficiently if there is insufficient camber. So, do you go softer or stiffer?

As tire technology has advanced, the answer has become clearer. The increased grip afforded by modern R-compound tires generates very high degrees of body roll in many autocross cars. It has become very common for front-engined autocross

Tires have an optimum operating temperature. On hot days, tires are often sprayed with water to keep them cool. On cold days, passive tire blankets are often used to keep the tires warm between runs. (Photo Courtesy Bryan Heitkotter)

cars to lift the one rear wheel completely off the ground in the middle of the corner. This high amount of body roll translates to more change in the orientation of the tire on the pavement, often resulting in the extreme outside edge of the tire doing nearly all the work. This is clearly not optimum for either performance or tire wear.

The high degrees of body roll that are common with modern tires

mean that fitting the car with a stiffer front sway bar is typically the preferred adjustment. The greater the body roll, the more effective a sway bar will be. Stiffening the front sway bar of a car with lots of roll reduces body roll, sometimes significantly. Less roll means that the tire can sit more squarely on the pavement. The change in front roll stiffness does work the front tires harder, but the gain in tire efficiency usually dwarfs the negative of the added load on the outside front tire.

Adding stiffness does help grip, but it's a diminishing return. Sway bars work based on absolute roll. With the body roll reduced, the next increment of change is less effective than the last. Combining this with the increased weight transfer on the front axle caused by the stiffer sway bar, it becomes easy to overdo the big front bar theory.

As increased levels of grip translate into the need for greater roll stiffness, it may be apparent that one sway bar doesn't meet all needs. What works on one pavement may

This Volkswagen demonstrates why controlling body roll is important to reducing run times. The heavy roll the car is experiencing in the corner translates into pretty severe positive camber for the left front tire. This tire can't work efficiently and understeer is bound to follow. (Photo Courtesy Bryan Heitkotter)

not be adequate on another. What works well in the dry may not be good in the wet. Fortunately, there's a solution. Many aftermarket parts manufacturers make adjustable sway bars. These bars can be adjusted to a variety of settings between nearly stock to super stiff. This adjustability allows drivers to fine tune their cars to the needs of a particular day, often between runs. It's not completely uncommon for a serious autocrosser to change sway bars completely from one day to the next, selecting a different bar from several that are hung on the garage wall.

Body roll and weight transfer also affect how much power a driver can use in a corner. For some cars, most notably those with open differentials, the weight distribution on the drive axle is critical to quick acceleration. Body roll and weight transfer "unload" the tires on the inside of a corner. For rear-wheel-drive cars, a stiffer front sway bar tends to help keep weight on the inside rear tire. A bigger front bar helps the car accelerate. For front-wheel-drive cars, a stiffer front sway bar results in more weight being transferred off of the inside drive

With modifications limited in the Stock classes, the front sway bar is an important piece of the tuning puzzle. The front sway bar is the only real method of controlling body roll and the use of stiff front sway bars is common. This car has a bar stiff enough to lift the inside front tire clear of the pavement. (Photo Courtesy Bryan Heitkotter)

The use of stiff front sway bars can be overdone. In this case, a Mazda MX-5 lifts a front wheel high in the air during a corner. The car is softly sprung and the pavement is grippy, but it would seem that the front sway bar might be too stiff. (Photo Courtesy Bryan Heitkotter)

This Neon is a front-wheel-drive car. The heavy sway bar being used here is reducing the load on the left front tire. When the driver applies the throttle, the left front tire will be apt to spin, hampering acceleration out of the corner. (Photo Courtesy Bryan Heitkotter)

wheel. A bigger front bar can actually hurt acceleration.

Finally, for those few cars out there that oversteer straight from the factory, there is little downside to stiffening the front sway bar. This both reduces body roll and reduces the efficiency of the front end of the car relative to the rear end of the car. These cars are also typically rear-wheel drive, so the bigger front sway bar also aids in acceleration. The best example of this is the Honda S2000. These cars, currently listed in A Stock in SCCA's Stock category, seem to follow the trend of "bigger bar equals faster car."

Dampers: Black Magic!

In a nutshell, Stock category shock tuning is about using the dampers the wrong way. With limited options for changing the behavior of a car, misuse of dampers has become vogue. It's not right, but in some cases it works. When it works for someone, everyone jumps on board and makes it popular.

The Stock category rules allow for the use of any damper that has the same geometric characteristics as the stock damper and has two or fewer external adjustments. In many

This Mazda Miata appears to be benefiting from dampers that are stiffer than stock. Even though the car is turned hard in this slalom, the car hasn't really leaned over. As the driver is ready to turn the wheel back the other direction, the car won't really lean much in this element. (Photo Courtesy Bryan Heitkotter)

This Mazda MX-5 is slightly later in the same element. The steering wheel isn't turned as hard, but the car appears to be leaning as much, or more, than the Miata. The stiffer dampers on the Miata reduce the body roll and make the car feel more responsive to steering input. (Photo Courtesy Bryan Heitkotter)

cases, aftermarket dampers meeting these criteria are easy to find. If Koni makes an off-the-shelf unit to replace your stock dampers, you're in business. Once you find a part, it is important to verify that the replacement part has the same geometry as the stock part. This involves checking the length of the shock body and placement of the spring perch, as well as measuring the length of the ears on McPherson struts.

Assuming you've found an acceptable part, what types of adjustments are common? Most dampers come as single-adjustable units. Koni has dampers for many applications that adjust only rebound damping. Higher-end units may have two adjustments; one for compression and one for rebound. There are several manufacturers making "budget" replacement dampers with a single adjustment that changes both rebound and compression at the same time. As previously discussed, compression adjustments are primarily used for adjusting to a different surface (bumpy or smooth), and rebound adjustments are commonly used to change the balance of a car. As a "buyer beware" caution, the quality of stock shocks on high-end sports cars has gotten to be very good. In some cases, fitting a car with off-the-shelf aftermarket "performance" dampers results in *reduced* performance on an autocross course. Not every car benefits from "upgraded" dampers.

That's the end of the conventional wisdom of shock tuning in the Stock category. From here on, it's all black magic. It has become common to use dampers to supplement the stiffness of the springs. Particularly on cars that are very softly sprung, very stiff dampers can limit body roll and significantly affect the balance of the car. To quantify how this works,

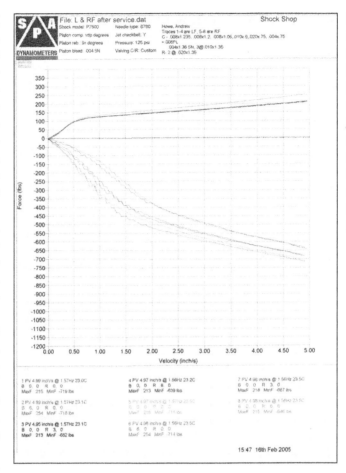

Shock dyno plot of a Penske 8100-series dampers used on the front of an A Stock Honda S2000. The various traces on the plot are force-versus-velocity curves for different settings of the external adjusters. Rebound damping is plotted below the x-axis.

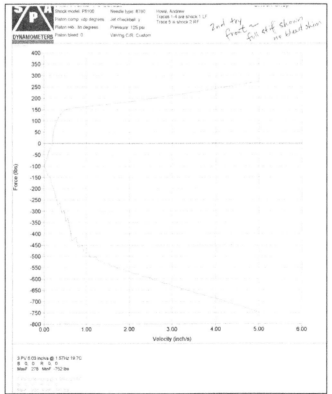

Shock dyno plot of the same Penske 8100-series damper as shown in Figure A. Internal changes to the damper have drastically revised the damping curve. In this plot, only the stiffest setting of the left and right front dampers are shown.

Stock class competitors can improve braking performance or brake bias by replacing the stock brake pads with higher performance units. The emphasis in autocross should not be placed on high-temperature performance, as brake temperatures seldom exceed those seen on the highway. As such, many race or track pads are inappropriate for autocross use. (Photo Courtesy Bryan Heitkotter)

The use of double-adjustable remote-reservoir dampers is legal in the Stock classes. Being legal doesn't make them a "must buy" item for the serious autocrosser, however. These dampers are very expensive and may only offer a small improvement over the stock shocks. (Photo Courtesy Bryan Heitkotter)

the damping characteristics of a shock must be analyzed and broken into three zones of motion: ultra slow speed, slow speed, and high speed.

- Ultra slow speed motions: These motions are the roll of the car at corner entry and corner exit of sweepers.
- Slow speed motions: These motions are the roll of the car in a slalom.
- High speed motions: These motions are associated with the bumps and dips of the pavement.

There isn't a hard break point between these three zones of motion. There is often overlap of velocities and tuning with dampers is always a compromise. To add to the frustration, manufacturers build off-the-shelf dampers to work the right way—that is to say they're focused on the high-speed motions only. As a result, adjusting a typical off-the-shelf damper does not often change the way a car handles in a sweeping corner.

So where's the magic? The magic is in high-end, custom-valved dampers. These units, typically from companies such as Koni, Penske, Moton, JRZ, and Ohlins, can be valved to a customers specifications. This allows the hardcore Stock category competitor to customize the behavior of a car to suit their needs. See the figures on page 94 for

examples of two damping curves from the same high-end damper. Note the differences in curve shape and damping rates.

These dampers are highly effective on some cars and completely irrelevant on others. In any case, they are very expensive and, for most drivers, aren't going to achieve much benefit. But the perception has gotten out that the high-end double-adjustable damper is required to win in some classes.

For those few who are going to take the plunge, the key to tuning with dampers is to focus on the behavior of each wheel at any given time on course. An adjustment to front-rebound damping is not terribly effective when the car is under heavy braking (the front dampers are being compressed under braking!). The last piece of the puzzle is to understand that all damping adjustments affect the car in more than one way. Be prepared to compensate for one adjustment with another.

For the average user and the off-the-shelf damper, rebound adjustments can be an effective way to improve the behavior of a car in a slalom. Increased damping rates generally make the car more responsive and feel more solid. If the car tends to oversteer in a slalom, increasing front damping rates tames it somewhat. If the tendency is to understeer, rear damping rates can be increased. If

Delays are inevitable at events. Here a worker is studying an instruction manual trying to get the timing and scoring system back up and running. When this sort of thing happens, just relax. The event will resume shortly. (Photo Courtesy Bryan Heitkotter)

The exhaust system is where Stock class competitors increase performance and save weight. With car manufacturers focusing on comfort more than performance, many stock systems are significantly heavier than they need to be. (Photo Courtesy Bryan Heitkotter)

the car skips or skates across the pavement, reduce the damping. And, as with the sway bars, less grip usually means less need for high damping rates. So, in the rain, feel free to try softer damper settings.

Exhaust and Other "Expendable" Items

I've grouped these together because modern automotive engineering has advanced to the point that performance gains from "miscellaneous" items are pretty small. They do exist and, with some research, you can narrow the field of

what is helpful for your car. In no case are these items the difference between winning and losing at the regional level.

That said, there are a couple popular items that can make a significant impact on the way the car performs: brake pads and exhaust systems.

Changing brake pads can be advantageous to the Stock category autocrosser. While the brake systems are generally off limits, the brake pads can be changed. If you want to slightly change the brake bias of your car, upgrading to a high-performance pad at one end of the car can accomplish this. If the brakes simply don't work as well as you'd like, upgrade all four corners. When shopping for brake pads it is important to remember that what works well at an autocross is completely different from what works well at the race track. Track pads are designed to work at high temperatures and are often very poor at the low temperatures of an autocross car's brakes. An aggressive, street compound brake pad is often the best choice for the autocrosser.

The one obvious "upgrade" that many consider worthwhile is the exhaust. I don't think very many modern cars see an increase in horse-

The use of a lightweight, high-flow exhaust system has disadvantages. The most notable compromise is more sound. The lighter exhaust will be louder than stock. On a car like a Corvette, a louder exhaust may push the car to the limits of the sound meter. (Photo Courtesy Bryan Heitkotter)

power or torque from an aftermarket exhaust, but that's not the only benefit of such a change. Many modern mufflers are very heavy. In the extreme case of replacing a twin muffler exhaust with a high-flow single muffler, the weight reduction can be significant—upwards of 30 pounds! This weight reduction can actually improve the performance of the car. The downside? The car will be louder because much of the weight reduction comes from removing baffles from the inside of the muffler. With comfort and noise restrictions (both on the street and at the event) being considerations, think carefully about this one before buying and installing.

Here is a bolt for adjusting camber. Note the offset between the head of the bolt and the threaded shank. "Crash bolts" are similar in look, but with a larger offset between the head and the shank than the stock bolt. The larger offset provides a wider range of adjustment.

While the Stock category is the lowest level of preparation that the SCCA offers, some competitors still have dedicated autocross cars. Can you imagine commuting to and from work in the Zebra? Dedicated cars like the Zebra can be beaten with a daily driver—you don't need to have a dedicated car to have fun and win. (Photo Courtesy Bryan Heitkotter)

The Factory Service Manual

How is legality of cars determined in Stock category? The rules point to the factory specifications as the standard for each car. The rulebook indicates that the Factory Service Manual is the primary manufacturer's documentation. In the event of a protest, the driver of the car in question must produce the Factory Service Manual for the car, so the Protest Committee can figure it all out.

That's the legalese of the matter. In reality, this typically is not required at regional events or by non-SCCA clubs. It is, however, a good idea to have the Factory Service Manual. This manual has a lot of good information about the vehicle and can be beneficial to determine what is and is not allowed. And let's face it, having the manual can be very helpful if you have a mechanical problem with the car, especially when you're away from home.

For those who have cars where the Factory Service Manual is not available to anyone other than certified service technicians, don't worry. The SCCA recognizes that this is becoming increasingly common. In this case, the SCCA does not require the participant to provide the Factory Service Manual to resolve a protest.

Bottom line: The Factory Service Manual, while expensive, is probably going to be a good buy. If it's available, buy one.

Mazda is an example of a manufacturer that has historically supported its racers. The Mazda Motorsports program gives competitors access to certain parts at reduced cost. Additionally, the program pays money to successful drivers at big events, provided they are registered in the program. (Photo Courtesy Bryan Heitkotter)

The Factory Service Manuals are not an exciting acquisition. It is, however, required documentation at SCCA National events. Aside from being bulky and expensive, this manual can help the competitor maintain the car. All in all, it's not a bad purchase.

Alignment

Enough about buying new parts. What about doing the best with what you've got? You've already used all the allowances in the rules to fix what ails your car and it's still not quite right. What do you do? You can use the techniques discussed previously to get the most out of the car.

There is no requirement for the alignment setting to be within factory specifications. The Stock category rules require that only factory-approved adjustment methods may be used, but allows that out-of-specification alignment settings resulting from the use of factory-specified techniques and parts are legal.

And to top it all off, there's the possibility of adding still more parts. Some automakers allow the use of "crash bolts" in the suspension of their cars to achieve the factory-specified alignment. These bolts allow a wider range of adjustment than the factory parts. If these crash bolts are specified as acceptable for noncompetition purposes in the Factory Service Manual, these parts are legal for use in the Stock category. If you have them available to you, you'll likely want to acquire a set. (See Chapter 4 for more specifics on alignment.)

With all of this in mind, use the tools the manufacturer gave you to maximize grip.

BEYOND STOCK: SUSPENSION AND LIGHT CHASSIS MODIFICATIONS

Once you move beyond the limitations of the Stock category, you have many tools available to tune an autocross car. The most significant of these modifications, in terms of time saved on course, will be in the suspension. The other convenient changes are bolt-on-type modifications to the chassis. Many of these modifications are both inexpensive and easy to make. A competitor progressing beyond the Stock classes can shave gobs of time on the autocross course without ever touching the powertrain.

Suspension Bits

Once you move beyond the Stock classes, suspension theory reverts to the "normal" concepts. The rules allow reasonable modifications that will allow most production cars to be quite a bit of fun. Most notably, camber adjustment is expanded to the point that a car can actually use its tires effectively. To go with this, springs, dampers, and rear sway bars become unrestricted allowing serious tuning of the suspension.

The general order of operations for tuning a suspension system is as follows:

- Select spring rates and ride height.
- Adjust alignment.
- Select sway bars.
- Optimize alignment.
- Tune dampers.
- Fine tune alignment (if necessary).

You can do the work out of order, but this order is generally preferred. Also, expect to find yourself going back to the first step from time to time. This is normal; it's all part of tuning.

The car's suspension geometry and spring rates determine the car's basic tendencies. From this point, the alignment should be set to make the tires work efficiently. The testing that determines the best alignment at this point also gives a good indication as to the correct sway bars to be used on the car. After the "correct" sway bars are on the car, the alignment will

Those who aren't satisfied with the performance of their car in stock trim can move up the preparation ladder. Street Prepared allows bolt-on suspension modifications and powertrain upgrades like aftermarket clutches, flywheels, and engine management. (Photo Courtesy Bryan Heitkotter)

Class Spotlight: Street Touring

Street Touring is a relatively new category of cars. These cars are street legal (a car that isn't street legal for mechanical reasons will violate one rule or another) and are allowed very minimal modifications to the drivetrain and little latitude in any area other than suspension. While the range of cars that are legal in Street Touring is still pretty narrow, the classes are very popular. With the exception of STS2, all cars in the Street Touring category are sedans. STS2 is restricted to small-displacement two-seat cars.

Aside from the limited preparation and restricted list of eligible cars, the primary feature of the class is the allowed tires. The class requires the use of true street tires (Treadwear of 140 or greater) and restricts tire width. This means that these cars are not only street legal,

In the Street Touring classes, competitors are required to use tires with a Treadwear rating of 140 or greater. This means that drivers can travel safely to and from events on their competition tires. (Photo Courtesy Bryan Heitkotter)

Street Touring S2 is a class specifically created for small-displacement two-seat cars. The rules are identical to Street Touring S, except that a different engine displacement limit is given and two-seat cars are permitted. (Photo Courtesy Bryan Heitkotter)

they can be driven to and from events in race trim. For the vast majority of the Street Touring competitors, the class is viewed as more fun than Stock and much more accessible than Street Prepared.

Unlike most other categories, Street Touring has different allowances, depending on the class, and a car can be legal in more than one class. The STS rules are the backbone of the Street Touring

rule set. They are the most restrictive and the remainder of the category is based on this set of rules with additional allowances. An STS car that takes advantage of the additional allowances afforded to STX competitors will be eligible to run in STX. Similarly, an STX competitor who exceeds the wheel or tire restrictions in STX but complies with the rules in STU is eligible for STU is eligable for STU.

How much fuel is in your tank? Weight does matter to an autocrosser, but excess fuel may not be a bad thing. Stock category cars can't improve the fuel system to make sure they can get all of the gasoline out of the tank while on course. Some models suffer from fuel starvation, or temporarily running out of fuel due to cornering forces. (Photo Courtesy Bryan Heitkotter)

In some cases, the only real difference between an STS car and an STX car is a differential. The Acura Integra GSR is legal in STS, but the Integra Type R has a mechanical limited-slip differential, which bumps it into STX. (Photo Courtesy Bryan Heitkotter)

Figuring out where to start when preparing a car can be the hardest part of the process. Once the car is prepared, the necessary adjustments are often much easier to figure out. (Photo Courtesy Bryan Heitkotter)

Sometimes it all feels good out on course, but the result just isn't good. Cones are often tipped over without the driver even knowing. This leaves the driver frustrated. Where was that mistake? (Photo Courtesy Bryan Heitkotter)

likely need some adjustment. With the springs and bars selected, the dampers can be tuned to help the car through slaloms.

Ride Height

A lower center of gravity reduces weight transfer. Lower is better, right? Not always. There are several things that weigh in when choosing ride height: center of gravity, tire clearance, camber curves, and effect on body roll, among others.

The first two effects are easy to quantify. A lower center of gravity is good. The car should be as low as possible without compromising other characteristics. Tire clearance is necessary. The car should be high enough that the tires do not rub the fenders.

The camber curve describes the camber gain or loss at the wheel due

This is absolutely as low as this Miata can go. Not only is the tire tucked well inside the fender, the front lip spoiler is almost dragging the pavement! (Photo Courtesy Bryan Heitkotter)

The ride height of a car must be high enough that the tires don't rub the fenders in a corner. This BMW has taken advantage of Street Prepared allowances to trim and flare fenders in order to be lower than would be possible with the stock fenders. (Photo Courtesy Bryan Heitkotter)

to suspension travel. This is only a function of the geometry of the suspension arms and struts. For a given suspension design, this curve is constant. The ride height of the car locates the starting point on the curve.

Normally, you would want the wheel to gain some amount of negative camber as the tire is moved in the bump direction, or upward into the fender well. This is because bump motions are commonly associated with the outside tire in a corner. The chassis usually rolls toward the tire, causing the tire to lose camber relative to the ground. The gain associated with bump motion reduces

the apparent camber loss caused by the body roll.

Similarly, you would like the wheel to lose some amount of negative camber when the tire is moved in the rebound direction or downward, away from the fender well. This desire is for a reason identical to that for gaining negative camber in bump: The change in camber helps keep the tire flatter on the pavement during cornering.

Last, the ride height of a car affects how much the chassis will roll in a corner. This is not entirely obvious at face value, but it is true. And, quite often, lowering a car increases chassis roll. The geometric property in play here is called the roll center and it is a geometric property of the suspension, much like the camber curves.

The instantaneous roll center of the suspension defines the point about which the chassis will rotate under cornering loads. The amount of body roll is related to the vertical distance between the roll center and the center of gravity of the sprung mass of the car. This distance is sometimes referred to as the roll couple but, while it is convenient, it isn't

    HOW TO AUTOCROSS

Bushings

The rubbery things in the suspension are called bushings. They help keep the ride quiet and soft on the highway. They also allow the suspension components to move a little bit, compromising the alignment settings and suspension geometry. Worse yet, they eventually wear out wreaking serious havoc on the performance of the car.

In SCCA Street Touring and Street Prepared categories, it is acceptable to replace the stock bushings with another non-metallic bushing. Most cars are equipped with bushings that are reasonably soft. It is easy to find replacement bushings that are made of a harder rubber or a stiff polyurethane material. These parts are often relatively inexpensive and easy to replace. And, when you're measuring alignment specs to tenths of a degree, it is worthwhile to replace the stock bushings with the good stuff.

Another quirk of SCCA rules is the allowance for offset bushings. This allowance is somewhat of a gray area, but it is commonly interpreted that the hole in the bushing material may be offset within the stock bushing housing. This allowance can be used to make modest improvements in suspension geometry.

A tall car like this Volvo wagon transfers a lot of weight in a corner. Without lowering the car, there is no way to reduce weight transfer. Body roll can be reduced by modifying the suspension—springs, sway bars, dampers, etc. (Photo Courtesy Bryan Heitkotter)

With a ride height this low, the springs need to be pretty stiff. With the front tires tucked inside the fenders when the car is parked, bumps and cornering loads could easily push the tire into the fender. Stiff springs will reduce the suspension travel, keeping this from happening. (Photo Courtesy Bryan Heitkotter)

The nose of this Toyota Celica dives under heavy braking at the finish of a course. Each time the suspension is loaded heavily, bushings are stressed. Once a bushing is worn out, the car can become unstable and braking hard could be an adventure. (Photo Courtesy Bryan Heitkotter)

Spring Rates

Once the analysis of the suspension geometry is complete and the ride height has been set, you can select spring rates. The spring rates need to be selected to control body motions and still allow the tire to follow the pavement. This means the springs need to be stiff enough to keep the body roll in check, but soft enough to comply with the bumps.

quite accurate. There are two roll centers for the car: one at each axle. The relationship between front and rear roll couples does affect the understeer/oversteer balance of the car. The location of the roll center or the size of the roll couple does not affect total weight transfer; this is only dependent upon the height of the center of gravity of the car.

Two pieces of information are very important to the selection of spring rates: the motion ratio of the spring (how much the spring moves when the tire moves) and the weight supported on that axle.

The third piece of information that is often relevant is the amount of lateral grip that is expected. More grip means the need for a higher spring rate to control body roll.

Typically, motion ratio is nearly fixed for a particular axle on a car, at least at lower levels of preparation. The weight on the axle typically does not change much with car preparation. So, you're left with the idea that a particular range of spring rates will be right for a given car. Exact rates are dependent upon driver preference and other details.

Sway Bars

Recall that sway bars are another way to combat body roll. Sway bars are generally not as effective as springs in combating roll, but they should be used to tune the car. The principles here are the same as in Stock category, except that both front and rear bars can be used.

Camber Adjustment:
Pandora's Box

For a good number of cars, the stock suspension doesn't have anywhere near enough camber adjustment to accommodate the needs of an autocrosser. Once you move beyond the Stock category rules, you have options to adjust the camber to a more appropriate setting.

The typical allowances are the use of camber bolts and either alternate suspension arms or camber plates, depending on suspension design. All of these tools will get more negative camber than stock, but each has side effects. Each of these changes adjusts the suspension

Class Spotlight: Street Prepared

The cars in Street Prepared are heavily modified in comparison to Stock class cars, but are still relatively unmolested. The word "Street" doesn't mean that these cars are street legal, however. While a majority of the cars in Street Prepared are street legal and street driven, there are several allowed modifications that might make these cars illegal for street use. The primary allowances in Street Prepared are generally derived from maintenance needs or common performance improvements. Suspension and light drivetrain modifications, as well as minor alterations to the bodywork, are legal. Wheels and tires are unrestricted, except that tires must be DOT legal.

The fundamental concept of Street Prepared is to take a car and improve on factory shortcomings without making the car completely useless on the street. In reality, the rules have changed a bit over the years, both in the rulebook and on the road. Allowances like the removal of catalytic converters change the nature of the car very little, but render the car illegal for street use. Street Prepared competitors need to decide if they are in it just for fun or to win a National Championship. Deciding this helps in choosing the appropriate level of car preparation.

The range of competitive cars in Street Prepared is pretty broad. In F Street Prepared alone, the Ford Focus battles with the Honda Civic with cars, such as this Triumph TR6 mixed in, to the trophies. (Photo Courtesy Bryan Heitkotter)

There's no disputing that Street Prepared can cost more money than Stock or Street Touring. But you don't need to have a heavily modified 911 GT2 to have fun, either. There's nothing in the rules that says you must use every allowed modification. (Photo Courtesy Bryan Heitkotter)

The use of stiffer springs or stiffer sway bars would reduce body roll on this Miata. Unfortunately, both of these changes would also compromise ride quality on the street. For those who can't afford a dedicated autocross car, these compromises must be balanced. (Photo Courtesy Bryan Heitkotter)

A Street Prepared category car can be modified in many ways. One of the major allowances is for using a non-stock rear sway bar. Installing an adjustable sway bar gives competitors one more means to adjust the car when at the event. (Photo Courtesy Bryan Heitkotter)

The McPherson Strut Problem

Camber adjustment on a McPherson strut car can be achieved in several ways. In Street Prepared, the methods are restricted to camber bolts and camber plates. An additional allowance permits the strut body to be offset farther from the hub by way of alternate strut geometry. In Street Touring, the rules allow either the use of camber plates and camber bolts or the use of an alternate lower control arm. Each method has its merits.

The use of a camber bolt allows increased negative camber with minimal changes to suspension geometry. This method, while maintaining the geometry as close to stock as possible, also pushes the top of the tire closer to the strut body and spring perch. The camber bolt allows relatively simple adjustment of camber.

The use of camber plates to achieve negative camber doesn't change the clearance between the tire and the strut body. It does, however, reduce the motion ratio of the strut, softening the effective spring rate at the wheel. The camber plate typically allows for the adjustment of camber and caster.

The use of an alternate lower control arm doesn't affect the clearance of the strut and is not terribly adjustable. The alternate lower control arm does, however, reduce the movement of the roll center due to changes in vertical wheel position. This method could be very effective with the development of a control arm that has independent adjustment of both the front and rear legs of the arm. This would allow independent camber and caster adjustment. This type of arm is not, however, common at this time.

McPherson strut cars are not known for having great camber curves, but at least the rules give you choices to improve the suspension. So, pick your poison.

geometry somewhat and may alter the camber curves and/or roll center locations of the car. While any of these methods are helpful; one may be more helpful than the others.

A specific item to consider when selecting a method of camber adjustment is caster. Caster may be changed when camber is adjusted, either by design or incidentally. This is an interaction to be aware of when selecting parts. If you want the ability to have caster adjustment, pick your parts accordingly.

Dampers

Once out of Stock class, a completely different set of circumstances controls damper selection. No longer are dampers being used to augment the stiffness of a suspension equipped with soft springs. Now dampers can be used as they were intended: to damp unwanted chassis and wheel motions.

Without resorting to boring math, a damper is a critical element in the suspension system. Without the damper, the wheel and tire (or the chassis) will bounce for a long, long time. This bouncing causes the

McPherson strut cars suffer from questionable camber curves. The solution is a lot of static camber. The result is shown here: The outside front tire is upright and working hard. The inside front tire has 6 or 7 degrees of camber, relative to the pavement—clearly not optimal, but about as good as it can get. (Photo Courtesy Bryan Heitkotter)

When a Mini is campaigned in the Stock classes, there are no legal means to get a reasonable amount of negative camber on the front axle. In Street Prepared, this isn't a problem. (Photo Courtesy Bryan Heitkotter)

contact pressure between the tire and the pavement to vary wildly—and with it, the size of the friction circle will vary wildly. This is clearly not a good situation.

The sprung mass of the car (chassis) and the unsprung mass of the car (wheel, tire, brakes, etc.) are connected by a spring. The body motions of the car and the irregularities in the pavement cause the two masses to oscillate relative to one another. Damping absorbs the energy of the oscillation, eventually stopping the motion and returning the system to equilibrium. There are three states that the system can assume based on the level of damping:

- Underdamped: the system oscillates for several cycles before stopping.
- Overdamped: the system never completes one oscillation.
- Critically damped: the system completes exactly one oscillation before stopping.

The physical characteristics of these states are that a severely under-damped spring allows the chassis or tire to bounce. A severely over-damped spring causes the tire to skip

Most racecars are classed unfavorably at an autocross due to the modifications required to make them competitive in their racing class. Spec Miatas are given a bit of a break. They are specifically classed in D Street Prepared, even though they have modifications that are not legal in the class. (Photo Courtesy Bryan Heitkotter)

across the pavement. A spring that is close to being critically damped performs as desired. In application, you generally use dampers that keep the system slightly overdamped to give yourself a car with quick response.

The behavior of the spring-and-damper system is dependent upon three things: the sprung mass, the unsprung mass, and the stiffness of the spring. The smoothness of the pavement helps you define how overdamped the system can be

before performance deteriorates. A rough pavement surface requires a spring and damper system that is close to being critically damped. A smooth surface allows highly over-damped systems to be effective.

Why bring all of this up again? To remind you that you don't need super-stiff, high-end dampers to have a well-behaving autocross car. While there is some tuning advantage to be gained by using the trick double- and triple-adjustable high-end dampers, the gains are small and the costs are high. If you think you're headed down this path, serious research is warranted before spending your hard-earned money.

In application, adjustable dampers should be used to allow for changes in surface roughness and variations in either the mass or spring stiffness of the suspension system. Dampers should not be used as a primary tuning tool like they are in the Stock classes.

Corner Weights and Cross Weights

Every car has a weight distribution that can only be adjusted by moving weight within the car. The front-to-rear weight distribution can only be adjusted by moving weight within the car. Left-to-right weight distribution has a similar problem. Once the front and rear weights have been adjusted as much as possible, you have one more tool available to you: cross weights.

Cross weights are the weight of the car measured on each diagonal. That is, the left-front plus the right-rear make one cross and the right-front and left-rear make the other cross. This is very important in determining how a car behaves. Most important is that folks who can adjust the ride height of their car can adjust the cross weights.

CSP might be heavily populated with Miatas and MX-5s, but they're not the only cars in the class. The Honda CRX and Toyota MR Spyder are also popular entries. (Photo Courtesy Bryan Heitkotter)

Strut systems don't have to be ridiculously expensive to be effective. The Eibach / Ground Control system is relatively inexpensive and does its job well. This system can be retrofitted to most dampers to make a fixed-spring system have an adjustable ride height.

The cross weights help determine how well a car turns right or left. Try this exercise: Draw four tires, looking down from above. Draw arrows from the rear tires to the front tires along the lines of the cross weights. One arrow points forward and to the left, and the other points forward and to the right. If the cross weights are unbalanced (not 50/50), the car will turn one direction more easily than the other. Specifically, the car will turn more easily in the direction of the heavier cross weight. If the left front and right rear are heavier, the car will turn left more easily than if the cross weights were even.

Cross weights are adjusted by changing the corner weights of the car. By raising or lowering one wheel, you can change the way the weight of the car is distributed to the tires. Raising a corner of the car adds weight to that corner. Lowering it reduces the weight on that corner. Because you aren't actually moving weight, the change in weight comes from an automatic adjustment of the weights on the tires of the other cross. That is to say, raising the right rear of the car increases the weight on the right rear and reduces the weight on the right front and left rear. By default, the weight on the left front is also increased. This is just like shimming a table that rocks.

By changing the cross weights, you can adjust how well the car turns right or left. It's important to note that this operation should be done with the driver's weight considered. It's also important to note that a 50/50 distribution of cross weights may not be desirable. Setting cross weights should be done with the left-right weight distribution considered. Recall that a car with more left-side weight (perhaps because of the weight of the driver) turns left more easily than it turns right. In this case, a cross weight setup that favors the right front-left rear diagonal may be favorable.

The final comment on corner weights and cross weights is to say

Cross weights can be adjusted by raising or lowering the spring at one corner of the car. A threaded body strut is a convenient way to make these adjustments. Raising the car adds load to that tire (and its cross weight); lowering the car has the reverse effect.

that every car with adjustable ride heights should have its cross weights adjusted. Despite your best efforts to install all of your parts perfectly, it is common for one corner of a car to be higher or lower than it should be. Even a small error (especially on cars with very stiff springs!) can significantly affect the corner weights. Consider this process a necessary final check of the ride height settings.

Summary

Overall, suspension tweaks are a significant part of the performance increase from Stock to Street Prepared.

Street Touring rules allow adjustable ride height. This gives the owner of this Subaru WRX the ability to make the car turn well in both directions. Even minor adjustments in cross weight can make a car more consistent. (Photo Courtesy Bryan Heitkotter)

Even a vintage ride with a somewhat archaic suspension design can be fast and fun. Classes like Open Street Prepared allow a little more latitude than SCCA's standard rules, making a wider variety of cars fun. (Photo Courtesy Bryan Heitkotter)

Rain tires work on slightly different principles than regular tires. On one hand, lower grip means that a lower tire pressure can be used, allowing additional adherence to the pavement. On the other hand, a higher tire pressure will resist hydroplaning better. (Photo Courtesy Bryan Heitkotter)

The allowances to customize spring rates and get adequate camber really enable competitors to fine-tune their cars. At the same time, the higher level of preparation will also reward deeper pockets and mechanical aptitude more than in a Stock class. With more allowances, competitors with more money have more avenues to spend it to improve their cars. Likewise, a setup wizard who's an average driver will move toward the top of the results sheet because his or her car will be faster than the competitors' cars.

Wheels and Tires

Bluntly put, use the widest wheels and tires that are legal and fit on the car. Well, run the widest tire that is legal and fits on the car and the most appropriate wheel width for that tire. Except in Street Touring, where there are also some wheel width restrictions.

Just because you can physically mount a 245/45/16 onto a 6.5-inch-wide wheel doesn't make it a great idea. It's the best idea in a Stock class, but not when wheel widths are less restricted. Tires work best when mounted on wheels that are approximately the same width as the tire. That 245/45/16 will be very happy when mounted on a 9-inch wheel.

The principle at work here is that a skinny wheel pinches the tire and forces the tread into a curved shape. A wider wheel lets the tire be in its natural shape—with a flat tread. The curved shape means the tire is not flat on the pavement and is not working as effectively as possible. It is true that for a given rim width, a wider tire is usually faster, but you're not really restricted in rim width anymore. Put the right wheel with the chosen tire.

Tire Diameter

When choosing a tire size, overall tire diameter should be a consideration. In Stock, this won't be much of an issue because there aren't a wide variety of tire sizes available. You are usually stuck with one or two choices. In other classes, you can choose between different wheel diameters and tire widths.

Tire diameter directly affects two things: tire-to-fender clearance, especially when turning, and the final effective gear ratio. The first item is

In Street Prepared, the allowances make it easy to run wide tires. No rule is in effect mandating that tires fit inside the fenders so trimming and flaring of fenders is permitted. Just fitting appropriate tires on a car can significantly improve performance over a Stock class car. (Photo Courtesy Bryan Heitkotter)

In the C Street Prepared battle, the MX-5 has an advantage in wheels and tires. The ability to mount a 285/18 tire on such a light car gives the car an advantage over its competitors. The Miata and CRX contingent have been recently helped by Hoosier's introduction of a 275/15 tire. (Photo Courtesy Bryan Heitkotter)

This C Street Prepared Miata is about as low as it can possibly be. If the driver switched to a larger-diameter tire, the car would need to be much higher above the pavement. Also, a larger diameter tire would have different gearing, meaning the driver's shift points would change. (Photo Courtesy Bryan Heitkotter)

This C Street Prepared Miata is using tires and wheels shorter than the stock size. There are several advantages to this (less unsprung mass, less rotating mass, lower center of gravity), but one key reason is the change in gearing. Using a shorter tire effectively results in a lower final drive ratio meaning more torque is put to the ground in each gear. (Photo Courtesy Bryan Heitkotter)

The combination of a custom wheel and a wide wheel spacer means that stock wheel studs likely won't be long enough. The use of long aftermarket wheel studs and open-ended lug nuts can solve that problem. It may not look great, but the alternatives are unacceptable.

relatively obvious: A larger diameter tire needs more space inside the fender wells. The second item is more complicated.

A larger-diameter tire has a larger circumference. The larger circumference means the car travels farther per revolution of the wheel and, in turn, the car goes faster at a given engine speed. The speedometer does not reflect this change. Connected with this is a change in effective gearing—second gear feels like "2nd and a half" and the car accelerates more slowly. A smaller tire diameter has the reverse effect.

It's a trade off. More speed in a given gear could keep you from reaching the rev limiter and allow you to make up time at the end of a straight. However, the taller effective gearing means you'll be giving up time under acceleration at the head of the straight. There's no universal right or wrong here, just one more thing to consider.

Wheel Spacers

Sometimes the tire of choice, when combined with the best available wheel, has some clearance issues. If the tire is rubbing the chassis inboard of the hub face, a wheel spacer can be fitted to the car to increase the clearance. This spacer fits between the hub face and the wheel and is held in place by the wheel and lug nuts.

The benefit of the wheel spacer is obvious, but it has some potentially serious side effects. These side effects are increased steering effort, increased wear on wheel bearings, and a reduction in available thread

Taking Care of Wheel Studs and Lug Nuts

Regularly swapping tires can cause wear and tear on wheel studs and lug nuts. Anyone who has broken a wheel stud knows that replacing it is a pain. The following tips can help keep breakage to a minimum.

Keep the lug nuts out of the dirt. When removing lug nuts, place them in a plastic bin for safekeeping. Keeping the nuts as clean as possible will minimize wear due to grit and dirt.

Regularly clean the threads. As you install and remove wheels, dirt and gunk is bound to get onto the threads, even if you're careful. Take the time to clean the threads of this dirt every so often.

Torque the lug nuts to the factory specification. The temptation is there to tighten the lug nuts to a torque higher than the factory specification. This will certainly keep them from loosening on their own, but it can also damage the threads.

Consider using an anti-seize compound to prevent wear and tear on the threads. This is a technique that is generally frowned upon by the engineers in the business, but it offers proven results. The engineers have a point, however. The factory torque specification is generally written for a clean, dry stud and nut.

Replace lug nuts regularly. This might seem excessive, but replacing lug nuts generally lengthens the life of the wheel studs. A new nut has near-perfect threads, a significant improvement over lug nuts that have been used dozens of times.

Hand start all lug nuts when tightening. The advent of portable drills and impact wrenches has undoubtedly caused a few problems over the years. These tools put torque onto the nut whether it is threaded properly onto the stud or not. Start the threading by hand to make sure it's right before putting a power tool to work.

A little bit of care when installing and removing lug nuts and wheel studs can save headaches. It is tempting to use drills and impact wrenches to save a little time when changing tires, but one cross-threaded lug nut ruins a day. (Photo Courtesy Bryan Heitkotter)

length on the wheels studs for the lug nuts. The change in steering effort is a nuisance, but you can live with it for a performance advantage. The wear and tear on wheel bearings is a maintenance item; bothersome but not a serious issue. The reduction in threads for the lug nuts is a serious safety concern, however.

Lug nuts and wheel studs (or hub bolts) are designed with particular parameters in mind. The most important of these is the length of threads that are engaged when tightening the lug nuts. This length determines the strength of the connection and how much force can be carried before the lug nut fails. Shortening the length of thread engagement reduces the strength of the lug nut. Period.

There are factors of safety in the original design, yes? Yes. How big is the factor of safety? How many threads to I need to have engaged to be safe? These are tough questions. Remember that the original design didn't involve dancing through cones on super-sticky tires. In the world of building design, a structural nut needs to engage a length of threads roughly equal to the diameter of the shank of the bolt. This rule-of-thumb is crude, but it is a place to start.

In application, a 12mm x 1.5mm thread pitch lug nut threads onto a 12 mm-diameter stud. To engage 12 mm of threads, the nut needs to be turned eight revolutions on the stud. For a 12mm x 1.25mm thread pitch, the number of revolutions increases to almost 10. Another option is to have open-ended lug nuts and engage all of the threads in the nut.

If you have a question about whether or not you have enough threads showing to be safe, buy longer wheel studs or hub bolts. It can be tough to find a part that works. In many cases, the manufacturer of the wheel spacers will be able to source and supply longer wheel studs for your application. If in doubt, err on the side of safety.

Lightweight Batteries and Battery Relocation

The rules permit the stock battery to be replaced with any battery of the same voltage. If your car is like every other car on the road, the battery is more than adequate for autocross. You seldom need that many cold-cranking amps on the solo pad.

In the interest of saving 10 to 25 pounds, replacement of the stock

Small batteries are a great way to trim a few pounds off a car. Most stock batteries weigh in excess of 30 pounds. Small aftermarket batteries, such as this Braille unit, often weigh 15 pounds or less.

Suspension parts are the most heavily stressed components in an autocross car. This hub broke under corning loads, sending the car spinning off course. It can be difficult to inspect components like hubs, but the consequences of a failure can be unacceptable and dangerous.

battery with a lightweight model has become common. There is only one real downside to this: A small battery won't run very many accessories with the engine off. When selecting a lightweight battery, it would be wise to consider more than just one's needs at the autocross course. Many an autocrosser has been seen with jumper cables and a dead lightweight battery.

Battery relocation is also permitted under the rules. This allowance permits moving the battery to any location that is not in the passenger compartment. At face value, it might seem beneficial to move the battery. Some nose-heavy cars have the battery parked way out on the nose. Moving that weight to the rear would be good for weight distribution. Don't forget the weight of wiring that will be added when relo-

cating the battery! Think about whether the relocation is worth the 5 pounds of heavy-duty wire that is needed to run to the back of the car. Maybe it isn't worth it anymore.

Race Seats

Installing race seats is a great way to improve performance. It isn't a bad way to lose some weight out of the car, either. Race seats hold a driver in place much more positively than most stock seats. Race seats are also, particularly with the advent of side airbags that are built into factory seats, generally lighter than their stock counterparts. The allowance covers the driver's and front passenger's seats.

The rules intend to allow common, full-size race seats to replace the factory seats. The rules allow any seat, fixed-back or reclining, to replace the stock seat, provided it is fully upholstered and has a headrest that is not below the middle of the driver's head. An additional requirement is that the seat be securely mounted using the stock mounting holes and that the seat, with all of its mounting brackets and hardware, weighs at least 25 pounds (20 pounds in Street Prepared).

This rule evolved over many years, as competitors exploited loopholes in the verbiage. First, small child-sized seats were outlawed. Then a minimum weight with mounting hardware was specified in order to prevent anyone from attempting to gain advantage from ultra-lightweight (and unsafe) seat mounts.

The improvement in seat design may mean that you no longer need your CG Lock or 4-point harness to stay in your seat. It may also mean that your stock seat belts don't work very well anymore. When choosing a seat, consider how the car will be

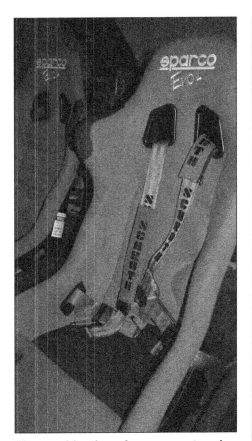

The combination of a race seat and a 4-point or 5-point harness is a great way to make sure that you stay firmly in your seat. In many cases, it is also a great way to reduce the weight of the car.

used and whether or not the factory seat belt system is still adequate. Some cars have a portion of the seat belt system mounted to the seat. And sometimes race seats aren't designed in a manner that easily permits use of the stock seat belt.

Remember, it should be safety first. The rules permit fitting aftermarket seat belts. Installing a race seat is a great time to consider something other than the stock belts. If the car is to be used both on the street and on the autocross course, it would be wise to consider a DOT-approved belt system. Systems that are DOT approved are legal for use on the highway. Schroth Racing makes belt systems, including their

Chassis Bracing

There are two dominant thoughts about chassis bracing in Street Touring and Street Prepared. First, chassis bracing isn't generally legal. Second, if your car will benefit significantly from the chassis bracing that is legal, you've likely got bigger problems. In Street Touring and Street Prepared, there are only two ways to legally stiffen a chassis.

The first, and by far the most common, way is to install a strut brace. A strut brace is defined as connecting left- and right-side suspension-mounting points, but only connecting an upper mount to an upper mount or a lower mount to a lower mount. This allows the competitor to prevent lateral distortion of

Strut tower braces are common enhancements to the chassis. This bar prevents some movement of the strut towers to maintain suspension geometry during heavy cornering.

the chassis at the suspension mounts. In most cases, modern cars have little chassis distortion in these areas. Benefits, if any, will be concentrated in the Street Prepared classes as the higher grip levels afforded by race tires generate proportionally higher levels of chassis distortion and flex.

The second way is to install a roll bar or roll cage. Legal roll bars and roll cages are well defined in the SCCA's rulebook. These structures stiffen a chassis substantially, dramatically reducing twist of a unibody, but at the cost of adding a significant amount of weight. A properly designed and legal roll cage will weigh in the neighborhood of 100 pounds. A roll bar or roll cage is generally a good idea for safety reasons, particularly if the car is used in track events as well, but don't look to a roll cage as a performance-enhancing modification in autocross.

A roll bar may not be considered chassis bracing by some, but it can significantly stiffen a chassis. For people who intend to use their car for both track-day events and autocrossing, installing a roll bar is a reasonable step. (Photo Courtesy Bryan Heitkotter)

Rallye 3 and Rallye 4 belts, which are legal for use on US highways.

Update/Backdate

SCCA's Street Prepared category has a very special allowance commonly referred to as update/backdate. This allowance affords competitors the opportunity to interchange specifications between cars. This permits a competitor to build a car that has the best attributes of all variants of car included in the allowance. Update/backdate is important to the serious SP-category competitor, but it is often confusing how it can be used and what constitutes a legal update or backdate.

Update/backdate can only be used to interchange specifications of cars listed together in Appendix A of the SCCA Solo Rules, Street Prepared classing. The limitation is written explicitly as "listed on the same line" of the Appendix. As an example, here is the D Street Prepared listing for the BMW 3-series sedans:

    2002tii (all)
    325 and 328 (E30)
    323, 325 and 328 (E36)
    330ci, 330i, 330cic (E46)
    3-series (16V NOC)
    Bavaria

Reviewing this listing, a BMW 325 built on an E36 chassis can interchange specifications with both the 323 and 328 models that are built on the E36 chassis. They can't interchange specifications with models built on either the E30 or E46 chassis, even though those cars are also in D Street Prepared. Those cars are listed on a separate line.

How do you interchange parts and specifications? The "new" part must be standard on the vehicle from which it was taken (factory options are OK) and the part must fit into the new car without any modi-

fication, aside from standard factory installation methods. Engines and transmissions or transaxles must be swapped as whole units. You can't take the heads from one car and transplant them onto the block from another, but you can have the whole engine.

Out-of-Production Cars

When stock parts are no longer available, what do you do? Manufacturers in the United States are only required to stock parts for a car for 10 years after its production date. After that, there is no guarantee that the part will be available. For older cars, this can be a problem.

The SCCA has an allowance in the Street Prepared rules that permits the substitution of non-stock but equivalent parts for out-of-production stock parts. The allowance has some catches—the replacement part

must be as similar to the stock part as possible—but the concept is very beneficial to competitors.

Street Prepared's update/backdate allowance legalizes interchanging specifications between particular models and model years. This car, originally equipped with a passenger-side airbag, was able to interchange specifications (and dash assemblies) to a model year that did not have the passenger-side airbag.

BMW's E36 sedans enjoyed a relatively long production run with several different engine variants used. The Street Prepared update/backdate allowance is very kind to this car for this very reason. (Photo Courtesy Bryan Heitkotter)

The mix of older cars and a requirement for stock parts presents a problem. The SCCA resolved this in Street Prepared classes by allowing older cars to use equivalent non-stock parts when the stock parts are no longer available. (Photo Courtesy Bryan Heitkotter)

BEYOND STOCK: POWERTRAIN, BALLAST AND AERODYNAMICS

Improving a car's suspension is the fastest (and often most cost effective) way to improve times on an autocross course. It is not, however, the only way to improve a car's potential. Powertrain, aerodynamic devices, and ballast are key concepts for many of the classes that allow higher levels of preparation.

Engine

Unlike in a lot of motorsports, power isn't everything in autocross. Having more power is certainly good, but it needs to be useful power. An engine tuned for autocross is very different from one that is tuned for peak power. I won't discuss the nuts and bolts of how to build the engine

Street Modified, Prepared, and Modified were created for people who like to work on their cars and make them fast. These classes are equally one part car preparation and one part driving skill. (Photo Courtesy Bryan Heitkotter)

Street Modified allows many common street modifications such as this carbon fiber hood. The class has evolved, but the original intent was to give the heavily modified but still potentially streetable autocross car a place to be competitive. (Photo Courtesy Bryan Heitkotter)

HOW TO AUTOCROSS

Class Spotlight: Street Modified

Street Modified cars are the most heavily modified "street" cars in Solo. In addition to SCCA's Street Modified class, many clubs have an Open Street class. The purpose of these classes is to allow for most common modifications to production automobiles without hacking up the chassis. In keeping with the "street" spirit of the class, nearly all of the extraneous factory parts (such as interior, windows, windshield washer systems, etc.) must remain intact. All seriously prepared cars in this category are illegal for highway use. The SCCA currently has two classes in this category: one for sedans and one for two-seat cars.

Street Modified allows all of the modifications from Stock, Street Touring, and Street Prepared plus its own list of allowances. The major Street Modified allowance that the lower classes don't enjoy is that the drivetrain is nearly unrestricted. Competitors can use any engine from the same manufacturer as their car, provided the engine could be fitted into the car without modifying the chassis. Suspension allowances now offer unrestricted choices for anything that moves when the wheel moves up and down.

Because this class is so wide open, I will not discuss modifications specific to this class. Street Modified car preparation delves into automotive engineering and books addressing that topic should be referred to for guidance for items not discussed here.

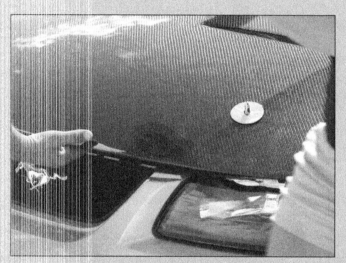

Street Modified allows many common street modifications such as this carbon fiber hood. The class has evolved, but the original intent was to give the heavily modified but still potentially streetable autocross car a place to be competitive. (Photo Courtesy Bryan Heitkotter)

Street Modified class cars bear a strong resemblance to their stock brethren. This BMW M3 is heavily modified, but it still clearly looks like an M3. This class requires drivers to maintain most road-going necessities, such as windshield wipers and headlights. (Photo Courtesy Bryan Heitkotter)

or what parts to use (that's another book), but I will cover what qualities are important and why.

A typical autocross course has lots of short bursts of acceleration. Speeds are low. It is very uncommon to have more than 200 feet of continuous full-throttle acceleration and the upper gears are seldom used. Another trait of the autocross course is the large amount of time a driver spends at partial throttle. This is in stark contrast to road-racing circuits or the drag strip where long runs of full-throttle acceleration are the norm.

The autocrosser will find three qualities of their engine very important. The first quality that is very useful is a quick throttle response. The second quality is a reasonably smooth and predictable power delivery. The third quality is a broad and useful torque curve. Peak horsepower isn't on the list anywhere. It is important, but it is worth sacrificing some peak power in order to make the power more useful.

Throttle Response

Throttle response is important to the autocrosser because the acceleration happens in short bursts. A driver in a car with good throttle response

This driver has taken advantage of the rules to improve breathing in his Honda S2000. This setup shows individual throttle bodies with a velocity stack for each cylinder. In Street Prepared, Street Modified, Prepared, and Modified, creativity is a key to success. (Photo Courtesy Bryan Heitkotter)

happen automatically. The supercharger or turbocharger needs to pressurize the whole volume of air from itself to the intake valves before the full effects can be enjoyed. The larger this volume of air, the longer this process will take. Large intercoolers can be a great way to reduce the temperature of the intake charge, but the large volume of air contained within the intercooler will lengthen the amount of time it takes to achieve full pressure. Similarly, a long run of tubing between the turbocharger or supercharger and the intake manifold will take longer to pressurize than a short piece of tubing. Throttle response can be improved by paying attention to these details.

The nature of tubrocharging systems is prone to lag and poor throttle response. A supercharger uses engine power directly to build manifold pressure. A turbocharger uses energy in exhaust gases, energy that would otherwise be wasted, to make manifold pressure. This means that a turbocharger isn't sapping power

is able to accelerate earlier and with more vigor than if he or she were driving a car that is slow to respond. Poor throttle response may mean that the car won't even be making a lot of power at the end of the short straight. With a quick throttle response, a driver can wait until the right time to start applying the throttle. With poor throttle response, a driver needs to apply the throttle earlier than it is needed and estimate when to accelerate and how much throttle is appropriate. Obviously, the second scenario requires a driver to be somewhat more conservative. The little bits of time lost at each corner can add up to a few tenths of a second—or more—over the entire run.

The modern, fuel-injected naturally aspirated car has a very quick throttle response. Forced-induction cars, on the other hand, don't always respond so quickly. Supercharged cars also commonly enjoy good throttle response. Turbocharged cars can have very poor throttle response. Development of forced-induction

engines requires some consideration be made to throttle response.

The nature of forced-induction systems requires that the intake charge be pressurized to make maximum power. The act of depressing the throttle doesn't cause this to

When you drive your car as hard as you can, heat can become an issue. Engine heat can sap power. This driver is using water and evaporation to cool his car's intercooler. A cold intercooler efficiently cools the intake air on turbocharged engines to make maximum power. (Photo Courtesy Bryan Heitkotter)

Noise Abatement

While most people think of racecars as being loud, some places require racecars to be quiet. Autocross venues are no different. When the neighbors don't appreciate the noise, clubs have to place restrictions on sound levels of cars. The most commonly used measurement of sound is decibels measured on the A-scale (dBA). A common method of measuring sound levels is to place a sound meter at a fixed location near a point of full-throttle acceleration, 50 feet from the course.

The current A-scale (ISO 226:2003) is weighted to best capture sounds between 600 Hz and 6,000 Hz, the ranges that most often correspond to engine noises. This is slightly different than the original A-scale, which was sensitive to higher frequencies and was sometimes affected by ultrasonic frequencies. The current scale is much more sensitive to sound between 2,000 Hz and 6,000 Hz than the original scale. If noise readings vary widely from club to club, it could be because one club has an older meter.

All talk of frequencies aside, if you have a noise problem you'll have to fix it. In locations with stringent standards, even a stock Corvette may have issues. The most acceptable solution is to install a quieter muffler. Temporary means of beating the sound police include adding inexpensive aluminum dryer-vent ducting to the end of the exhaust system. These are commonly pointed down into the pavement or (somewhat defeating the spirit of sound enforcement) pointed horizontally away from the sound meter. If none of these methods seem to work, you can lift off the throttle at the sound meter to reduce the meter's reading. To reiterate: The most acceptable solution is to install a quieter muffler.

Why the need for temporary measures? There is more to noise than just what comes out of the car's tail pipe. Changes in atmospheric conditions can alter sound readings significantly during the course of a day. Denser air transmits sound more easily. Fog and low clouds can reflect sound to the ground. Cold and humid conditions are the best for transmitting sound, especially when aided by low cloud cover. A variation of 5 dBA is not uncommon from morning to afternoon.

When sound is a problem, sometimes you need to improvise a solution. This Corvette uses a turn-down at the end of the muffler to reduce the apparent sound levels. In a pinch, all sorts of dryer-vent solutions have been created at an event. (Photo Courtesy Bryan Heitkotter)

from the engine to pressurize the intake. It also means that the engine has to generate exhaust gases before there is power to be used. Another quality of turbochargers is that a larger turbocharger—capable of building higher manifold pressure—requires more power from exhaust gases. It takes time to generate exhaust gases from a change in throttle position. This time is called turbo lag. The common solution to this problem in racecars is called anti-lag. Anti-lag systems create pressure and energy in the exhaust by adding fuel directly to the exhaust system between the engine and the turbocharger.

Power Delivery

Smooth and predictable power delivery allows a driver to apply throttle with confidence. Smooth and predictable power delivery means the engine delivers power to the wheels in a manner that doesn't upset the car. The common, naturally aspirated engine does this very well. Unfortunately, as you strive to add more top-end power, you can introduce hiccups to the system.

Automakers have taken to building dual-purpose engines for their sports cars and sport sedans. These cars are being built with fuel economy and high horsepower in mind. This often leads to a car with a split personality. Dr. Jekyll at low RPM and Mr. Hyde when wound up. The two most obvious cases of this are the use of variable valve timing and variable lift systems and the use of

The Honda S2000 is a classic example of a car with two distinct attitudes. Below 6000 rpm, the car is very benign. Above 6,000 rpm, the engine screams. Unfortunately, the transition between the ranges is rather harsh, often making the car difficult to control. (Photo Courtesy Bryan Heitkotter)

The Formula 500 cars in F Modified have a very narrow power band. Fortunately for them, their rules have them using a continuously variable drivetrain. The system is tuned to keep their small displacement engines at or near peak power at all times. (Photo Courtesy Bryan Heitkotter)

turbochargers. In both of these cases, the car can be tuned for fuel economy and power.

When tuning a car with these features for autocross, it will often be advantageous to tweak the transition between economy and performance. The addition of power to the economy range is clearly beneficial on the autocross course. The removal of power from the bottom of the performance range may be beneficial as well. While removing power reduces the performance potential of the car, a more predictable car is often easier to drive, giving the driver more confidence and allowing the driver to be closer to the limit. Each car and driver is different, so be sure to test extensively on course if you're trying to work on this aspect of the engine.

Torque Curve

Everyone talks about peak power, but that's not what is important on an autocross course. An autocross car spends around 45 seconds on course per run. Less than 5 seconds of this will be at or near peak-power output of the engine. On the other hand, around 15 seconds will be spent accelerating hard at lower powerlevels. More importantly, the peak-power seconds are seldom at the important beginning of the straight.

The fact that autocross courses are typically run in first and second gears mean that very few gear changes are made. Most cars have little overlap between these gears. A particular speed will clearly be in one gear or the other. This means that the engine is asked to work across a wide range of RPM. The amount of power an engine has at 6,000 rpm is

In spite of your best efforts, sometimes mechanical gremlins arise. Heavily modified cars seem to have more problems than Stock class cars. Fortunately, their owners are often familiar with how the car works and what needs to be fixed.

C Prepared class cars typically don't have a shortage of torque. With a lot of displacement at their disposal, second gear is typically the only one that is needed. Having torque available at 3,000 rpm means that a driver doesn't need to think about downshifting. (Photo Courtesy Bryan Heitkotter)

Prepared and Modified class cars are engineered for maximum performance. Part of this is selecting gear ratios so that the available power is used as effectively as possible. These cars are far from stock trim and adjusting gear ratios can yield significant improvements. (Photo Courtesy Bryan Heitkotter)

A very high-horsepower front-wheel-drive car can benefit from a limited slip differential. It won't work wonders, however. With enough power, a driver can easily spin both drive wheels. (Photo Courtesy Bryan Heitkotter)

of little importance when trying to accelerate at 4,000 rpm.

How broad is broad enough? The answer is determined by the spread in gear ratios between first, second, and third gears. In order to downshift, the engine speed in the lower gear needs to be both safe and useful. Downshifting to first gear so you can hit the rev-limiter half a second later isn't useful. Pick the maximum engine RPM in the lower gear that is useful when downshifting into that gear and translate that to a speed. Now take that speed and translate it to RPM in the higher gear. This is the lowest engine speed that you think you'll use on an autocross course. Give yourself a buffer of a few hundred RPM and tune for torque from there to redline. This should cure most of the frustrations of full-throttle lack of acceleration.

Differential

In the land of autocross, an open differential is a bad thing. With the car being driven through corners most of the time, the drive wheels are seldom all solidly planted on the pavement. This uneven load makes it pretty easy to spin a wheel when trying to accelerate. Unfortunately, because you're turning the car in very tight corners, the drive axles can't be locked, either. The locked differential promotes understeer in tight corners. Enter the limited-slip differential.

Each car has slightly different needs, but just about every autocross car will be fine with about any style of limited-slip differential. These units come in three general varieties that are described as 1-way, 1.5-way, and 2-way differentials. All of these units act to distribute torque when accelerating. If there is no additional coupling on over run, the differential is 1 way. The 1.5-way differentials are designed to distribute torque under lift throttle, but allow a substantial

Sitting inside the frame of this A Modified car is a sealed limited-slip differential (gold colored). With a chain drive, the sealed, standalone differential is the perfect answer. It minimizes wheelspin while still allowing the two drive wheels to turn at different speeds. (Photo Courtesy Bryan Heitkotter)

Class Spotlight: Prepared

The Prepared classes are designed for production cars that have been modified heavily. These cars don't even pretend to be street legal and many are anything but race ready. Prepared class cars fall into two categories: XP and the rest of the cars. XP is like Street Modified, but with even more allowances. The rest of the classes are more in line with Street Prepared, but with more allowances. In Prepared, most of the extraneous running gear can be removed from the car and it can run on any tire that fits on the legal wheels for the class.

Like Street Modified, Prepared is more about engineering than simple car preparation. In many cases, Prepared category competitors even fabricate their own parts. It would be worthwhile to consult others with similar cars, as well as racecar engineering references, before undertaking major work on your car.

A Prepared was the home for cars prepared in excess of their class allowances, but within the overall Prepared ruleset. With some evolution, this became X Prepared. X Prepared allows significant creativity in car preparation and engineering. (Photo Courtesy Bryan Heitkotter)

E Prepared cars may have started life as relatively sedate autos, but E Prepared is not sedate. As a rule, E Prepared is filled with lightweight cars that are heavily modified from their stock configurations. (Photo Courtesy Bryan Heitkotter)

This is a Subaru WRX transmission and front differential. In the case is the stock front differential, an open unit. Next to the case is a brand-new limited-slip differential.

amount of slip. A 2-way differential is designed to be distributing torque all the time. The common thinking is that a 1-way or 1.5-way differential is the best choice for the autocross environment. Some folks like the feel of the 2-way units in rear-wheel-drive cars.

The most common pitfall of limited-slip differentials is excessive slip. For a Torsen differential, this is caused by having one wheel off the ground—the design of this differential requires some resistance for it to function properly. For differentials where the locking action is caused by a clutch pack, excessive wear causes the differential to slip heavily. In fact, just about every design has some sort of compromise. Research will help you figure out what compromise you want to make.

Ballast

You've already established that you want your car as light as possible. Why would you add ballast? Street Modified, Prepared, and Modified classes have minimum weights.

Rules in some classes allow modifications at a price. Sometimes a wider wheel comes with a weight penalty. Sometimes a larger displacement engine requires a higher minimum weight. In this case, it is the carbon fiber bodywork. These rules push competitors to think about ballast. (Photo Courtesy Bryan Heitkotter)

How to Ballast Without Ballast

What if your class doesn't allow ballast where you need it? It complicates matters a bit, but you can still move weight where you want it. When the location of ballast is restricted by the rules, you need to use other rules to move weight within the car. This is specifically true of SCCA Street Modified class rules; though it is likely other organizations have similar ballast rules.

The basic principle here is to take advantage of provisions in the rules that allow addition or replacement of components. Strategic use of allowances such as addition of subframe connectors in concert with legal weight removal in another area of the car can keep a car at a legal weight and move weight within the car. The real caution here is to not make it obvious that the component is acting as ballast—

overtly using such an allowance for ballast will generally run afoul of clauses that state the allowance "may serve no other purpose."

Here are some other possible ways to add weight to a car without needing ballast:
- A battery with a larger capacity is generally heavier.
- Mounting brackets for non-OE seats can be fabricated from steel rather than aluminum. They can also be beefy.
- A larger fuel tank may be fitted into the car.
- Stereo and speakers may be replaced for "comfort and convenience."
- A roll bar or roll cage may be added to the car (Note: this alternative is more about chassis stiffening than relocating weight).

Sometimes adding ballast is required to make sure that a car is legal for competition in these classes. And, as long as the car has to weigh a certain amount, you might as well use the ballast to your advantage.

Every car starts with its own weight and weight distribution. That is the nature of that particular car. Front-engine, front-wheel-drive cars are typically heavy on the front axle. Left-hand-drive cars are typically heavier on the left side due to the weight of the driver and controls. That's just how it is and you have to accept it.

In classes without a minimum weight, the recipe is simple: Remove as much weight as possible within

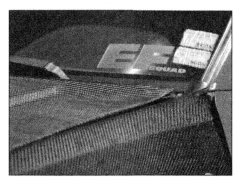

the rules. This rule still applies to classes with minimum weights, but the rules limit how much weight can be removed from the car. If a car is at its minimum weight for its class, no more weight can be removed. But that doesn't stop you from moving weight within the car.

The use of lightweight body panels on this car enables the owner to remove weight from the front of the car. If the car is above its minimum weight, the car gets lighter. If the car is below the minimum weight, the owner can add ballast in the back of the car, further changing its balance. (Photo Courtesy Bryan Heitkotter)

Moving weight within a car can be accomplished by removing weight from one area of the car and adding weight to another area of the car. This weight is typically added in the form of steel weights bolted to the chassis and it is called ballast. Ballast is cheap, but it's not free.

While significantly limited by class rules, the wing phenomenon has made its way into the Street Touring classes. The jury is still out about whether or not the use of wings in Street Touring is really of any benefit. (Photo Courtesy Bryan Heitkotter)

Testing has proven that the use of a spoiler is helpful at autocross speeds. This has lead to a proliferation of spoilers wherever they're legal and wings are not. It doesn't take a lot of downforce to change the behavior of an autocross car at high speeds. (Photo Courtesy Bryan Heitkotter)

In an A Modified class car, typically weighing less than 1,000 pounds with driver, generating a few hundred pounds of aerodynamic downforce is a significant benefit. (Photo Courtesy Bryan Heitkotter)

Why would you want to spend money moving weight within a car? There are three common reasons: First, you want to lower the center of gravity of the car. Second, you want to distribute the weight differently on the axles (move weight left to right or front to rear). Third, you want to reduce the polar moment of inertia of the car by moving weight closer to the middle of the car.

Lowering the center of gravity of the car means removing weight high in the car and replacing it with ballast that is low in the car. Lowering the center of gravity is important because a lower center of gravity equates to less weight transfer and body roll. This allows your tires to work more efficiently, including the ability to run with less static camber.

Distributing the weight of the car differently on the axles means you can use your tires more effectively. If a car has a heavily loaded axle or tire, it may be advantageous to remove some weight from that part of the car and add it back at the other end. Moving weight from front to rear on a car is

A racing car such as this is designed for high speeds. The aerodynamic devices on this car are of little use on an autocross course. Autocross-specific aerodynamic devices are tailored to high downforce without any real regard given to drag. (Photo Courtesy Bryan Heitkotter)

one way to reduce the demand on the front tires. Similarly, moving weight from left to right can help offset the effects of the driver sitting on the left side of the car and help the car turn right as well as it turns left.

Reducing the polar moment of inertia of the car by moving weight toward the center of the car makes it easier to initiate and stop rotation of the car. A car is like a flywheel. The

higher the polar moment of inertia of a flywheel, the harder it is to rev up or slow down an engine. Similarly, a higher polar moment of inertia means it takes longer for a car to respond to a driver's steering input. Quicker response is good in autocross.

Aerodynamics

In autocross, aerodynamics is often considered of little consequence. The speed of cars on autocross courses mean that aerodynamic effects are much lower than on a racetrack. Anyone who's driven a van on the freeway knows that air does move things at highway speeds. Autocrossers have started applying this knowledge when preparing their cars.

Class Spotlight: Modified

For those who are into tinkering, the Modified classes have some real bargains. These classes are significantly faster than Super Stock, but are generally far cheaper to run (A Modified being the real exception to this statement). Of the six traditional Modified classes, three of them are based on Club Racing cars (B Modified, C Modified, and F Modified); one is based on special-built cars specifically for autocross (A Modified); and two feature production-based cars (D Modified and E Modified). In addition to these classes, the SCCA has recently added Formula 125 for 125-cc shifter karts, though not all sites allow the running of karts.

The biggest bargains of the autocross world are in C Modified, F Modified, and Formula 125. These classes are the second (F125), fourth (C Modified), and fifth (F Modified) classes in autocross. C Modified is the most expensive of these classes, but

Formula 125 has become very popular in recent years. The combination of low cost, high performance, and small size make an attractive combination. (Photo Courtesy Bryan Heitkotter)

Modified class cars are essentially full-blown racecars. With this comes all of the troubles of a full-blown racecar. The cars require more specialized maintenance than production-based cars. The cars are also more difficult to climb in and out of. (Photo Courtesy Bryan Heitkotter)

cars can still be bought for less than $10,000. These classes are low cost because the basic vehicle has been in use for many years and the rules allow little innovation that hasn't already been worked out. Also, these vehicles tend to have more than one purpose, making them an even bigger bargain. A competitive C Modified car doesn't require significant work to be a viable Formula Ford road racing machine. Similarly F Modified is made up of Formula Vees (modified slightly to be more competitive) and Formula 500 vehicles. The Formula 125 karts can pretty much roll off the autocross course and onto a kart track. For someone who is interested in going racing, these vehi-

SCCA Club Racing cars can generally find a home at an autocross event. This D Sports Racer is legal to compete in B Modified. Being able to compete in both venues allows a driver to "graduate" from autocross into road racing. (Photo Courtesy Bryan Heitkotter)

Old autocross cars don't die, they just move up to Modified. This Lotus, owned by Ron and Karen Babb, is one of the most successful cars in SCCA autocross history. It has won in Street Prepared, Prepared, and Modified. (Photo Courtesy Bryan Heitkotter)

cles can be both a great bargain and a great transitional tool.

With the exception of A Modified, the remainder of the classes are also a bargain when considering speed versus dollars. B Modified is made up of Formula Atlantic and D Sports racers, among other cars. Outdated versions of these club racing cars can be competitive in Solo with some modification. These cars are more expensive than C and F Modified cars, but

Class Spotlight: Modified CONTINUED

they're also faster. D and E Modified cars are often very expensive vehicles, but they don't have to be. For the budget-minded autocrosser, these cars can be developed to something less than National Championship specifications and still be fast and fun. Additionally, D and E Modified cars often have little value outside of Solo. This means that often a competitive D or E Modified car can be purchased for a fraction of the cost to build it.

A Modified is the odd duck of Solo. These cars are referred to as "Specials" and have only one purpose: scaring cones. The wide-open rules of A Modified encourage the creative builder to push the limits of what is possible. These cars have a minimum weight of 900 pounds with driver and most of the restrictions are dimensional rather than technological. The suspension and drivetrain are nearly unrestricted and the wings are limited to a meager 20 square feet of area. In short, the top A Modified cars are the Formula 1 of Solo. For those who have seen a

A Modified is as fast as it gets. The latest generation of A Modified cars are unbelievably fast. These little machines can be more than 10 seconds faster than a Super Stock car on a 50-second-long course. In a slalom, drivers are limited by how fast they can turn the steering wheel rather than how fast the car can go. (Photo Courtesy Bryan Heitkotter)

well-developed A Modified car, the experience is moving.

Each class has its own clientele. The folks who enjoy Modified don't mind working on cars. Most of these classes are low technology by legislation. This keeps costs down, but there's not a car in these classes with anything vaguely resembling a Factory Service Manual or warranty. Also, none of these cars are street legal, requiring a tow rig and trailer to get to and from events. This keeps many drivers from joining the Modified classes. But for those with the desire and the resources, the Modified classes can be very rewarding.

While Stock category rules prohibit aerodynamic changes and Street Touring and Street Prepared severely limit creativity with aerodynamics, the allowances in Street Modified, Prepared, and Modified can be very useful. The allowances in these classes typically include front and rear spoilers and, in some classes, wings.

As a general rule, the most successful aerodynamic devices take advantage of the full extent of the rules. The benefit of such devices at autocross speeds is very limited. The cars don't move fast enough to make a lot of downforce. The low speeds also mean that aerodynamic drag is not a significant concern. As a result, exploiting the rules to the fullest extent has become popular. This means using a 10-inch-tall spoiler on a Street Prepared class car or the full 8 square feet of wing on a Street Modified class car.

Aerodynamic devices are effective for adding grip at high speeds. A device mounted to the rear of the car, like a wing, adds rear grip at high speeds. Such a device has little effect at lower speeds and no beneficial

When developing a car that is designed to have wings, one stage of development involves driving the car without the wings. The information gleaned at this stage can help develop mechanical grip, which is important at all speeds. (Photo Courtesy Bryan Heitkotter)

Adding wings to a car will do little to change its low-speed characteristics. Wings generate downforce based on their air speed. As the car speeds up, the downforce increases. Aerodynamic drag increases as well, but drag is not a significant consideration at autocross speeds. (Photo Courtesy Bryan Heitkotter)

effect at the front of the car. Similarly, a front splitter or spoiler only affects front grip at high speeds. These characteristics are important when choosing to add an aerodynamic device; adding a front spoiler won't help a car that oversteers at high speeds.

For most autocrossers, aerodynamics is a highly technical area of study and is nearly black magic to many. A technical discussion of the subject would take many pages and the mathematics would be very difficult most to comprehend (author included!). This leaves two ways to help make decisions regarding aerodynamics: Use the advice of others or get an aerodynamics modeling software package. The best advice here is to look at what successful folks are trying and use their knowledge. They can't hide it.

Tuning a Car with Wings

The addition of wings or spoilers to a car affords a little more flexibility in tuning. Aerodynamic grip is a great supplement for the mechanical grip generated by the suspension and tires. It's not uncommon to have a car that understeers at slow speeds and oversteers at high speeds. Recalling that aerodynamic devices are only effective at high speeds, the addition of a wing at the back of the car can help cure the high-speed oversteer without significantly affecting the low speed understeer. You can now (to a certain degree) tune the car separately for low-speed and high-speed elements.

The next step is to recognize that the addition of aerodynamic grip will likely require you to revisit your suspension setup. Let's face it: Adding grip is good. But let's make the most of it. If, for example, a car is very well behaved at high speeds but understeers miserably at low speeds, the addition of a rear wing may not make sense. It's still the right thing to do. Adding the rear wing will make the car understeer at high speeds as well as low speeds. While it may not seem that this is an improvement, it is. At this point, making a suspension change—a change to mechanical grip—that reduces understeer improves the handling at all speeds.

Formula 125 karts have exceptional mechanical grip. These karts are extraordinarily fast on an autocross course without the aid of wings. But, even the karts can exceed the limits of adhesion. (Photo Courtesy Bryan Heitkotter)

GETTING HELP

Once you've been hooked by the sport in a competitive way, you'll feel the drive to get better. Few drivers are natural talents. For the rest of us, improving takes time and lots of work. There are a handful of "shortcuts" to jump ahead on the learning curve.

Autocross can make a driver feel like a hero, at least for a moment. Improving on your own is very rewarding, but sometimes the pieces don't all fall into place. Before you become too frustrated, look to others for help. (Photo Courtesy Bryan Heitkotter)

Driving Schools

Using a driving school is the most obvious way to improve your driving skills. Driving schools are not a cure-all, but they are likely the single most cost-effective way to improve your times. This is espe-

cially true of first-year autocrossers. There are lots of schools available and research is necessary to find the best fit for you. Schools emphasize different things, offer different levels of instruction, and have widely varying costs.

Autocross Schools

Autocross schools come in two distinct levels of instruction: schools designed specifically for novices and schools for more experienced drivers. The former generally focuses on getting the driver around the course more efficiently and teaches the basics of course working and other key working skills. The latter variety of school focuses almost exclusively on going faster and teaching the finer points of the sport. Drivers are expected to provide their own vehicle at virtually all autocross schools. Additionally, the vehicle must provide seating for two.

Many clubs offer novice schools, and nearly every SCCA region with a Solo program has at least one school every year. If you are in your first season of autocross and want to get more into the sport, signing up for

There are lots of autocross schools out there. Each school has its own focus. Novice Schools held by local regions are intended to get the beginning driver started in the right direction. Schools like the Evolution School are for experienced drivers who want to improve their skills. (Photo Courtesy Bryan Heitkotter)

one of these schools is a good idea. Novice Schools have instructors from the host club to offer tips and pointers, and instruction can be somewhat tailored to an individual's needs. To get the most out of a novice school, be sure to contact the organizer and tell them your goals for the day. This allows the organizers to better match an instructor to your specific needs.

Costs of Novice Schools vary from region to region, but expect the cost to be around twice that of the region's regular event entry fee. Currently, the price would be in the neighborhood of $50.

To many folks, the other type of school begins and ends with Evolution Performance Driving Schools. The Evolution schools carry a hefty price tag, over $200 for a one-day

class, but it's worth it. Evolution hires experienced instructors from around the United States. Every instructor is a top-notch driver and many of their instructors are SCCA Solo National Champions. The Evolution program has several layers of instruction and it is common for students to take a particular class a second time. Each class focuses on slightly different topics, but every student starts with Phase 1.

To get the most out of Evolution, bring a car you are familiar with and fresh tires. You will get a lot of seat time and instruction. Also, expect to step aside and have your instructor show you how it's done. It's been said that stacking Evolution schools back to back can be good or bad. Some students love having the second day to reinforce the first day's lessons while others complain that it's too much information in a short time.

Evolution Performance Driving Schools are held around the country. Local clubs contact Evolution and host the event. Evolution provides the instructors. It is common for Evolution Performance Driving Schools to be held in conjunction with SCCA National Solo events, but

For people new to the sport of autocross, finding the course can be a daunting challenge. There are so many cones on the pavement, finding the right ones can be difficult. A Novice School can help you get your feet under you. (Photo Courtesy Bryan Heitkotter)

One snag for people wanting to take autocross schools is the need to have a second seat. Nearly all autocross schools want the instructor to be in the car with you. Not only that, they want the instructor to be able to drive your car and show you how you might improve. Drivers with single-seat cars need to look for a rental. (Photo Courtesy Bryan Heitkotter)

An Evolution School can significantly improve a driver's skills. With classes that sharpen a driver's line and teach the fine points of how to get around an autocross course quickly, many Evolution School students finish in the trophies at SCCA National level events. (Photo Courtesy Bryan Heitkotter)

Evolution Performance Driving School's bumper sticker, "Now I Suck Less," is a good way to look at learning. No school is going to turn an average driver into a National Champion overnight. Getting the most out of a school means having realistic expectations. (Photo Courtesy Bryan Heitkotter)

Tirerack, BMW CCA, and the SCCA have teamed up to create the Street Survival program. This is a driver's school for teens. The format is similar to an autocross setting and the idea is to teach young drivers proper driving skills in a safe setting.

many schools are held independent of SCCA event weekends.

Non-Autocross-Related Driving Schools

There are many different kinds of driving schools out there. While schools that aren't focused on autocross will not be helpful on subjects like finding the fastest line around the course, some of these schools can be very helpful with car-control skills. Often, their mantra for improvement is: "Seat time, seat time, seat time." This does hold true. Many cities have defensive driving schools that emphasize car control in adverse weather conditions. These can be a good deal for drivers needing to work on the basics of car control, which are similar whether the surface is wet, dry, muddy, or icy. Good schools to attend would be ones that use "skid cars" to simulate changing road conditions. These cars have special systems attached to them to reduce the amount of grip that is available to the driver. Spending time in very low traction situations helps hone the skills needed to autocross well and highlights bad driving habits that need to be broken.

Having a Co-Driver

Autocross events typically allow two drivers to drive the same car in a single class. Sharing a car with another driver, a co-driver, has many advantages. Co-driving can help improve times at a single event.

Having a co-driver in the car is a great way to improve driving skills. Comparing run times gives immediate feedback about what worked and what didn't work. This gives the "team" twice as many runs on the course to figure out the best technique for their car. (Photo Courtesy Bryan Heitkotter)

With two drivers in a car, necessities like tire changes are more easily handled. The schedule of an autocross event doesn't allow infinite time to deal with car issues. A second set of hands that is familiar with the work that needs to be done can be a real benefit. (Photo Courtesy Bryan Heitkotter)

Co-driving can reduce expenses. Co-driving can increase autocross knowledge in both car setup and car control. There are many reasons to have a co-driver and the best arrangement varies widely with the needs of the people involved.

With two drivers competing together in the same car, the initial benefits are obvious. Autocross, by nature, is about adapting quickly to the current conditions. Without any practice and (generally) only getting three runs to put down a fast time, any edge is important. With two drivers collaborating in the car, they can learn from each other. Each driver benefits from what they learn on their own runs and what their co-driver learns on their runs, too.

The economic benefits of co-driving can also be large. The costs of entry fees can be insignificant relative to the costs of preparing a car and traveling to and from events. For the autocrosser interested in traveling, having someone to split the fuel and hotel costs with can be a large benefit. Similarly, having a co-driver who is willing to offset some of the costs of preparing the car can mean the difference between autocrossing one more weekend or not.

The most significant benefit of having a co-driver is having someone constantly around to learn from. This can take several different forms in both car development and driver education. The whole point of this type of arrangement is to learn. The best way to do this is for each party to clearly understand their role in the partnership.

Getting the most out of the arrangement requires that you know how you want to improve. Each person brings specific talents to the event and shares that with his or her co-driver. Taking a superior driver on as a co-driver and instructor will help you improve your driving skills. Taking on a master mechanic and tuner will help your car perform its best. Even looking for something as simple as someone who walks the course better can improve your skills. This can shorten the learning curve and rapidly improve your autocrossing skills.

Each driver of the partnership needs to bring something to the deal. The exact terms of co-driving

Sharing a car with a season-long co-driver is a great way to improve your skills and reduce costs. With a co-driver, certain fixed costs, such as travel, can be split. The cost of a fresh set of tires can be split. All of these details need to be negotiated, but the right deal is beneficial to both parties. (Photo Courtesy Bryan Heitkotter)

Without eyes in the back of his head, this kart driver likely has no idea that he clipped this cone. Having someone else watching, an impromptu driving coach, can help a driver find small things like this. A change in line at this cone is necessary, but without help the driver may never know it. (Photo Courtesy Bryan Heitkotter)

At some point, every driver hits a plateau. Then it becomes difficult to improve. If you never ask for someone else's advice, how will you know where to improve? Ride with someone or have them ride with you. (Photo Courtesy Bryan Heitkotter)

arrangements vary, but both partners need to be happy with the terms. Some arrangements are purely economic with the second driver paying for the privilege to drive the car. Some arrangements are purely educational with the car owner allowing the mentor to drive the car in exchange for instruction. Some arrangements are purely related to the demands of research and development. Most are a combination of these types. Regardless of the reasons, a co-driver relationship can only work if the parties get along well and can reach a satisfactory agreement.

Free Advice

It might sound odd, but there is such a thing as good, free advice. Everyone who has enjoyed this over the years can give thanks to the general kindness and generosity of the autocross community. There are a couple big hurdles for those looking for free advice, however. You have to figure out whom to ask. You have to know the person well enough for him or her to donate time to help you. You have to know what kind of help you are trying to get.

All in all, it is easier to buy advice. But if you can get a good relationship going with other autocrossers, you'll find that free advice can also be easy to get and is often more meaningful than the advice you might buy.

Driving Skills

You've noticed a driver in your local club who is consistently one of the fastest drivers. How do you get that person into your car to critique your skills? How do you get into the passenger seat of his or her car to see him work his magic? The obvious way is to ask. It can be that simple, but most of the time it is a bit more complicated.

The first big step is being involved with the club enough so that your chosen instructor knows you on a personal level. No matter

For a novice driver, finding help is pretty easy. Most drivers at an event can point a novice in the right direction. Once a driver has been around the course for a season or two, it gets harder. Sharing a car with a driver who has different strengths can be one way to improve certain skills. (Photo Courtesy Bryan Heitkotter)

Research is important before traveling to attend an event with a new club. Lots of little things vary from club to club. Everything from event schedule to cone penalties might be different from that to which you've grown accustomed. (Photo Courtesy Bryan Heitkotter)

Using a helper is a great way to find a driving mistake. A driver, especially a beginning driver, is so focused on driving the car that small line errors can be overlooked. After the run, a passenger can use a course map to point out where the line can be improved. (Photo Courtesy Bryan Heitkotter)

how nice someone is, he'll always give more time and energy to a well-known cause. There's a decent chance that the club's biggest talents are also hard workers or organizers. Getting to know these people by pitching in goes a long way toward helping them remember who *you* are rather than just knowing "that's the guy in the Camaro."

Now that your instructor-to-be knows who you are, you'll also likely know him well enough to understand the best times to ask. When looking for one-on-one driving advice outside of a school setting, the key is asking at the right time. Being sensitive to your potential benefactor's needs can go a long way to helping your cause. If a driver is in the middle of competing, particularly if it is an important event, the response isn't likely to be enthusiastic. A similar request made after the conclusion of the event (or even over a beer) will often get a warmer response.

Once you've gotten a promise of help, make the most of it. Be specific about what you want and be willing to give something to get it. Typical offers include sharing your car at an event or paying the instructor's entry fee. At the event, try to walk the course with your instructor. Pick his brain about his intended line and any aspect of driving the course that interests you. Similarly, when the event starts, have him ride with you. Ride with him. Use the time between runs to glean what you can from him. If they are driving your car, be sure to ask pointed questions to improve specific points of your technique.

Another great way to get information about another driver's technique is to record his or her runs. This is especially helpful if you happen to be sharing a car. The recorded information can be used later to help you learn the differences between what you are doing and what your instructor did.

Car Setup
There are billions of places to get advice on car setup. OK, that's an exaggeration, but you get the point. Not all of the sources have the same information. How do you know what information is good and what information is bad?

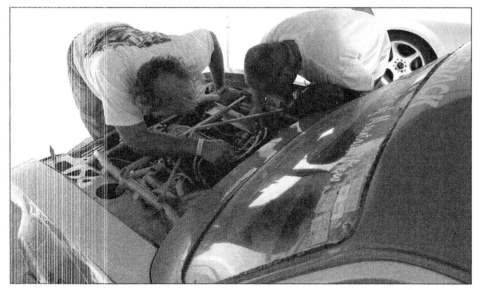

Finding good help can be critical to having a good time. Someone with experience working on your model car (or a similar car) can be a savior at an event. (Photo Courtesy Bryan Heitkotter)

The use of a spotter is commonly required when taking photographs out on course. A photographer is so focused on what is happening in the viewfinder that he or she often don't know what's going on around them. The spotter is responsible for seeing what the photographer doesn't. (Photo Courtesy Bryan Heitkotter)

The most important thing about taking information from other people is to know your source. Setup advice can come from people with many different backgrounds. Some of this advice will be helpful and some will be just plain wrong, even if the person giving the advice means well.

When seeking advice, find people with experience in applications that are as close as possible to your problem. Start with people who understand your make and model. Try to narrow the field further by limiting it to autocrossers. The next cut is to look for people with cars that have been similarly prepared. If you're really lucky, there will be a well-known and talented autocrosser who knows something about what you are trying to do. General information is good, but when it gets right down to it, specific experience is more important.

By far the best source of setup advice involves putting another driver in your driver's seat. To do this, coordinate with another driver in your area who is both a skilled driver and experienced with car setup. In this situation, the person giving advice is driving the car in exactly the same conditions as you are. Their feedback about how the car behaves will help you build confidence in your own skills to evaluate your car. His or her information about how to adjust the car will help you understand which modification will affect the car in what way. Most impor-

tantly, the advice will be based on first-hand knowledge of how your car behaves.

How to Get More Seat Time

To be honest, during the peak season, an autocrosser can find an event nearly every weekend. This isn't true everywhere, but it's true in enough places to make it worth mentioning. And, if you can't get enough seat time autocrossing, there are some alternatives.

In an effort to get the most seat time possible, be prepared to drive some distance to events. Participating in events hosted by several different clubs can get you significantly more practice than only attending events hosted by a single club. By being willing to travel a bit, you also learn which clubs put on the best events and where the best autocross sites are located. The downside to this approach is that you need to be able to invest a significant amount of time and money in the sport.

In order to get the most out of your autocross season, try these tips: Make a schedule that includes all of the clubs that are convenient. Invest

With the advent of Formula Junior, autocrossers can begin honing their skills earlier than ever. With proper approvals and insurance paperwork, some clubs allow drivers as young as 8 years old to participate in autocross events. (Photo Courtesy Bryan Heitkotter)

in a set of tires that will last for many autocross runs. Attend event weekends that give the most opportunity to be on course.

If there's not enough autocross in your area to suit your needs, there are alternatives. To be honest, driving anything at the limit will improve driving skills. Not all of the skills that are learned are directly applicable to the autocross, but some of the skills are useful. And, you'll probably be having fun.

Rallycross

Rallycross is similar to autocross and it's catching on around the country. Rallycross events are run on courses made of cones in an open space (sound familiar?). The big difference is that rallycross events are held on slick surfaces, such as grass, dirt, gravel, or snow. In a suitable vehicle, rallycross is a great way to get seat time and hone the skills needed to quickly adapt from one situation to another.

Karting

Anyone who says karting is a waste of time has never spent any time in a kart. First, many autocross clubs permit karts to participate in their events. Second, seat time in a kart often comes in 10-minute chunks. Third, with the advent of indoor karting, you can get into a kart year-round. The kart may not feel much like your car, but there are definitely some crossover skills. Places that rent karts often have underpowered karts that punish errors in control or line.

Data Logging

Autocross is a series of short runs. During these runs, you are too busy driving the car to analyze everything that is going on inside the car.

Camera Mounts

A camera mount has to perform two important tasks: It must hold the camera steady enough to capture quality images and it must not fail. Camera-mount design has varied wildly over the years, but a few things ring true for all systems.

Have a safety strap. In the event that the primary mount fails, a safety strap can really pay off. In addition to keeping the camera from flying around and being beaten into little pieces, it keeps the camera from injuring anyone. Cameras mounted to

A bird's-eye view of the course can help show the course. Properly framed, this angle should tell a driver whether the driven line was good or bad throughout the course. (Photo Courtesy Bryan Heitkotter)

Here's another innovative camera position. This angle can show a driver just how close the car is to the cones, but it can't give a perspective on the course or give any helpful indication about driving errors. (Photo Courtesy Bryan Heitkotter)

the inside of the car can fly around and cameras mounted to the outside of the car can be come flying objects for courseworkers to avoid.

Have the ability to adjust the camera about all three axes. This adjustment comes in very handy when the camera is "almost" pointed in the right direction.

Mount the camera in an out-of-the-way place. The camera should not impair the driver's vision or movements in any way. Driving the car is the first priority and logging video is secondary. Cameras have been mounted in a number of interesting places, but mounted to the windshield might not be the smartest choice. When mounting the camera in the car, consider the length of the safety strap. Mount the camera in a location that makes for easy starting and stopping of the recording. The last thing a driver needs to be concerned about when approaching the starting line is whether or not he can reach the camera.

A friend is not a camera mount. While it might seem like a good idea to bring a friend along to hold the camera, it isn't. If something unexpected happens, the camera can become a weapon bouncing around inside the car. Or worse, what if the airbag deploys in an accident? (Photo Courtesy Bryan Heitkotter)

All camera angles aren't created equal. This location is unique, but it also doesn't offer much information about how good or bad the driver's technique might be. The strap also needs to be attached to the car to make sure the camera doesn't fly off while on course. (Photo Courtesy Bryan Heitkotter)

This data typically comes in three distinct forms. The first is video recordings of the run. The second is logging horizontal acceleration data (g-loading). The final method is to record data directly from the car. It has gotten less expensive to log data and as a consequence, data logging is much more common than it used to be.

Video

Video is arguably the most important tool for beginning drivers and is definitely helpful for experienced drivers. Video cameras are typically used in three manners: mounted inside the car, mounted to the exterior of the car, and handheld or tripodmounted, operated by a second person watching from alongside the course. Regardless of the type of video, the important part of the equation is the time spent analyzing the video. Spend the extra time to look at it closely, as the important details are often subtle.

Mounting a camera inside the car is probably the most helpful use of a camera. This camera can be mounted in a manner to capture driver steering input and gear selection, as well as the course. Capturing driver input is key to observing driving habits and identifying issues to be corrected. This video often helps a driver identify issues like not using two hands on the steering wheel or giving harsh input. In addition to this, the camera offers some view of the course and gives an idea about the driver's line. This type of video is most helpful when two drivers are sharing a car, as it can clearly identify the differences in driving styles at different places on the course.

A video camera mounted to the car typically gives a better view of the course and car placement than a camera that is mounted inside the car. The obvious drawback is that this camera can't capture driving habits. Still, the camera mounted on the car is likely to miss some information about how well the car was placed because this camera has a fixed angle. Cameras mounted on cars have become more popular lately with the advent of the small camera that writes to flash memory. These can be easily secured to the car, adding little weight.

Video taken by another person often gives the best indication of how the car was placed in a particular element. The primary disadvantage of this method of recording video is that an autocross course is often large enough that the camera position does not adequately capture the entire course. The advantage of this type of video is that it takes no special mount.

Accelerometers and GPS Units

The use of accelerometers and GPS tracking units has become very popular in the 21st century. These systems are capable of plotting the car's position around the course as well as reporting g-loading at any given moment. These tools are incredibly useful for comparing two runs. For autocrossers with co-drivers, the data that is logged can show the team where time was gained or lost. For drivers who are consistent enough, the tools can be used to evaluate car setup changes.

The original logging systems were accelerometer based. One of the first really popular autocross accelerometer

The over-the-shoulder camera position is a great way to capture both the course and the driver's inputs. This angle should be able to capture steering angle and hand position, as well as identifying shift points. (Photo Courtesy Bryan Heitkotter)

Data logging to show position and speed doesn't require tapping into the car's electronics. This makes data-logging devices portable. Without any fixed device in a car, a driver can move the equipment to a second car in minutes to record additional information. (Photo Courtesy Bryan Heitkotter)

systems was the Geez!. This device used two accelerometers that could log data into a palm device or directly into a laptop. The acceleration data was processed using initial conditions input by the user to plot the position and speed of the autocross car. The data produced, while somewhat crude, showed drivers how well they used the friction circle and where they were underdriving the car. This system performed very well and is still useful, though seems a bit archaic today.

With the addition of more global positioning system (GPS) satellites in the sky, the technology has taken a different turn. More satellites available for use by a GPS device means faster and more accurate readings. Now, a car's path can be measured directly and accurately. Software writers took advantage of this. You have access to this tool that can continuously record a car's position on course and process the data to compute speed and acceleration. This system is easier to use than the Geez! tools of old; it requires less user input and calibration for accurate results. The leading GPS-based family of systems right now is MaxQData.

Technology has finally progressed to the point that data can be easily analyzed between runs. The MaxQData systems can be coupled with a pocket PC allowing for review of data almost immediately. This quick access to data can tell a driver immediately whether or not a particular portion of the course was driven better or worse than the previous run. A MaxQData unit that can record data at 10 Hz (this should be considered the practical minimum data acquisition rate for autocross) can be purchased for under $500.

Technology has the potential to change the approach to the three-run event. Drivers can now approach their final run knowing with certainty where they need to go faster. They have the ability to see *where* they are gaining or losing time on the course. The use of the latest generation of GPS devices in tandem with recorded video can quickly speed up a driver's learning curve. Soon, GPS units will be nearly as common on the grid as tire pressure gauges.

Direct Data Logging

Direct data logging consists of pulling information directly from sensors attached to the car. While you commonly think of engine and speed data, many systems can be monitored. Tools are available to log data on just about every automotive system that you might want to tweak. The ability to log data directly from an autocross car is strongly tied to how much money you are willing to spend. If you have access to the equipment, by all means use it. However, at this time, there are usually more cost-effective ways to improve your performance.

With A Modified being the pinnacle of autocross technology, these cars are often heavily instrumented. It is very common for the people working with these cars to be logging data on performance of several systems at a single event. They learn more about their car in three runs than many people learn in a season. (Photo Courtesy Bryan Heitkotter)

GOOD THINGS TO KNOW

A little research can make traveling to other clubs easier. Sites and club rules and procedures vary widely. Even things as simple as course marking conventions change. This course design gives the "sea of cones" look, but the course likely makes perfect sense to the locals. (Photo Courtesy Bryan Heitkotter)

Many people feel that it isn't possible to get the most out of autocross just by attending events and having fun. To these autocrossers, the basic flavor of the sport is enriched by experiences they get outside of the normal hometown event. Whether it is competing with someone in another class based on "indexed" times or competing with folks from other clubs, these folks get more out of the sport by opening their eyes and seeing what else is around them.

Traveling to Other Clubs

For those who want more seat time or want to try something new, the best way to do that is to travel to events that are hosted by clubs other than your home club. Not only does traveling give the opportunity for more seat time, the variety afforded by seeing another club's course designs helps the learning process. There are several tips that can help make traveling to another club less stressful.

Learning about the club's typical operations is the single most important thing that you can do to make the trip fun. Is pre-registration required? Do they have a special policy regarding minors on site? Are passengers allowed? What classing

Castle Airport's Winton Ramp was one of the greatest autocross sites ever seen. This site was huge and flat, paved in concrete. In addition to its enormous size, the concrete pavement presents most newcomers with a new challenge. Knowledge of the site is worth a good chunk of time on course. (Photo Courtesy Bryan Heitkotter)

There are lots of good reasons to travel to out-of-town events. The most compelling reasons are for good competition, better event sites, and more runs. Other reasons to travel to events would be to combine an autocross event with some other activity, such as a vacation. Regardless of the reason to travel to out of town events, make a list of those clubs that are fun. You'll want to keep going back for more.

The PAX/RTP Index

Many clubs that use the SCCA classing structure also use supplemental classes that include more than one class of car. These supplemental classes include Novice classes and Street Tire classes. Often the top competitors in each class use this index to compare their times to each other. Each of these clubs must use an indexing system to compare the times from each competitor in these classes. Rather than creating their own index, most of these clubs use the PAX/RTP Index, which is produced by Rick Ruth, long-time SCCA Chicago Region autocrosser.

system do they use? Do they have sound restrictions? Do they use the standard SCCA penalties? Is the event site large or small? The answers to these questions are important for setting expectations. There are two easy ways to learn this information: Ask someone you know who runs with that club or contact the event organizer.

Once you've decided that you want to travel to another club and know what to expect, make the most of it. Focus on learning things that you don't typically see at your home club's events. Because different people design courses for different clubs, expect to learn how to drive a different type of element or recognize a different set of visual cues. If the club you've chosen to visit has a top driver in your class, make the most of the opportunity to visit with him or her and see how you compare. If the pavement is different from the sites that your home club uses, learn something about how to adjust your car to suit that surface. Most importantly, be a good guest. Follow the club's rules and have fun!

The driver's meeting is crucial for folks attending an event with a new club. At this meeting, the "down and out" penalty rule is being explained. While most clubs use the same rules about cone penalties, some do use different rules. (Photo Courtesy Bryan Heitkotter)

All clubs need help putting on events. If you travel to an out-of-town event and find the hosting club needs some help, pitch in. The fastest way to win new friends in the autocross world is to be willing to volunteer when no one is asking for help. (Photo Courtesy Bryan Heitkotter)

Travel does add some difficulties. For those with sports cars, traveling to out-of-town events means finding a way to fit all of their stuff into the car. Or it means buying a trailer. Either way, the commitment to the sport is greater than it is for the autocrossers who only runs home events. (Photo Courtesy Bryan Heitkotter)

Originally, the PAX and RTP indices were separate entities. The first PAX Index was produced for 1994 and was intended for use by national-level autocrossers to compare times across classes. The RTP Index was first produced in 1995 and was intended to be more appropriate for local clubs. This original distinction between the indices makes sense—the relative speeds of the

classes is dependent on course type. In 2002, the indices were combined and the combined index is now based on results from a large number of clubs around the United States.

The creation of the index values for each year is a long process. The index is usually published in the late fall after the SCCA Solo Nationals and early enough for clubs to incorporate the changes prior to the year's competition. There are three major components in the value. The first factor is the set of index values for the previous year. The second component is the large volume of data that is collected from event results during the previous year. The final component is an educated guess about the impact of any rules changes or new technology that will be in use for the new year.

The most common misconception about the PAX/RTP Index is that it is intended to be used to equate cars. This is simply not the case. The purpose of the Index is to equate classes. The data collected to create the index is grouped by class. The data that is used to establish the value

Formula 125 is typically very fast. The class benefits from a very small size and light weight. As a result, the PAX/RTP index for this class is very high. A higher index—closer to 1.000—equates to a need to run a faster time to score the same after the index is applied. (Photo Courtesy Bryan Heitkotter)

for a single class likely captures several different makes and models and certainly captures many different individual cars. The data is analyzed to determine how fast the fastest car in the class could be on any given day. Some data is excluded from analysis due to known aberrant course conditions (rain, dirty course, etc.) Some data is given more weight (known high-quality

The PAX/RTP Index compares classes of cars rather than individuals. The fastest cars and drivers in the sport set the standard for each class. When competing against other drivers on the Index, you are really racing against the fastest cars in your class. Street Modified 2 class competitors are really racing against Andy McKee when their times are adjusted by the index. (Photo Courtesy Bryan Heitkotter)

While the PAX/RTP Index rates each class in a general sense, it is not a judgment about what class is faster on any given day. It is not considered legal to run a car in a "faster" class unless the car is actually legal for that class. In this case, the Subaru Impreza WRX STi should be running in B Street Prepared, not A Street Prepared. (Photo Courtesy Bryan Heitkotter)

drivers in well-prepared cars). The result is an approximation of how fast the fastest car in the class might be with the fastest driver.

The first step is to establish the fastest class based on the data available. This class has an index of 1.000 and is the baseline for all of the other classes. To date, the fastest class has always been A Modified. An adjustment of a class' index is indicative of a change in that class' performance relative to A Modified. If, in the future, A Modified is eliminated as a class, the new fastest class becomes the baseline.

After the baseline class has been established, the remainder of the classes are compared to this class. One class at a time, the data is analyzed. The analysis of all of the information for a class culminates in a single factor that approximately equates the fastest car in the class on any given day to the fastest car in the baseline class (A Modified) on that same day. Not all data is considered equally, as the drivers are not all equal in talent. Variations in course

The PAX/RTP Index is computed based on normal course conditions. For course designs that are abnormal or inclement weather, the PAX/RTP Index is not a good way to compare the classes. An example is that Street Touring cars have their index based on the use of street tires. Rain doesn't force them to change to treaded tires. (Photo Courtesy Bryan Heitkotter)

design and pavement surface are not normally considered when determining Index values. The Index is supposed to be reasonably accurate for most events regardless of course design or pavement surface.

Now that the PAX/RTP Index values have been established, you can use them. The Index value for the

Many local classes use the PAX/RTP Index. Some clubs have special "PAX" classes where the strongest drivers in the club beat up on each other. Some clubs have indexed Street Tire classes where competitors with different class cars, all of them on street tires, can compete with each other. (Photo Courtesy Bryan Heitkotter)

class is intended to be used as a multiplier to compare the class to the baseline class. Take the time and Index value for the run in question and multiply them together. This gives a time for a comparable performance by a car and driver in the baseline class. This is commonly referred to as the "Indexed Time." The lower the Indexed Time, the better the performance by the car and driver. To convert from Indexed Time back to a raw run time for a class, divide the Indexed Time by the Index value for the desired class. The result is the raw time that is equivalent to the Indexed Time in question.

The key feature of the PAX/RTP Index is that it equates classes, not cars or drivers. Each class index is based on the fastest car and driver in that class in the country—the standard for the class. The true purpose of the Index is to compare each car and driver against their standard, much in the way that "Best in Show" is determined at a dog show. The closer a car and driver perform to the expected standard, the better their Indexed Time is, relative to other

National Tour and Divisional events are typically attended by lots of autocrossers. With lots of cars around, the grid is a crowded place. Everyone has an assigned grid spot to help ease the clutter and confusion. (Photo Courtesy Bryan Heitkotter)

cars and drivers. A great driving performance in an under-prepared car does not give a good Indexed Time. Neither does a great car being driven with less than top-notch skills. A great Indexed Time can only be achieved with both pieces in place.

SCCA Divisional and National Tour Events

The SCCA has several levels of competition that correspond to the organizational structure of the club. The lowest level, the common event attended by beginners, is the Regional event. These events are the least complex and best serve the casual autocrosser. For those who have been seriously hooked by the sport and want to broaden their horizons, the SCCA has Divisional and National Tour events. These events attract autocrossers from several different regions and commonly draw large numbers of drivers.

SCCA Divisional and National Tour events are similar in nature, but distinctly different events. Divisional events are organized by a host Region with the assistance of other

clubs in their Division. National Tour events are organized by a host Region with the assistance of SCCA National Staff. Both events follow the same format and are organized to mimic the procedures that are followed at the SCCA Solo National Championships. In short, it's much more structured than Regional competition. But don't let that intimidate you.

Both Divisional and National Tour events have two days of compe-

A National Tour event gets the support of the SCCA National office. The timing and scoring equipment, course radios, and impound equipment travels the country. This same set of equipment is used to run ProSolo events. (Photo Courtesy Bryan Heitkotter)

tition. Each day follows a format similar to a Regional event with a different course being driven each day. The event results are based on adding the fastest single run from each day. In short, to win one of these events requires having two good days in a row.

Other than the obvious difference of being a two-day event, the difference between Regional competition and a Divisional or National Tour event is pure procedural. The entries are split by class into run groups and given work assignments. Registration, Technical Inspection, and a Driver's Meeting are taken care of before the event begins and are not significantly different than a Regional event. The differences come in three places: grid, course working, and impound.

The Grid is different at a Divisional or National Tour event because everyone has an assigned grid position. Grid positions are assigned to ensure that everyone runs in the correct order. At these events, cars in a class are run consecutively to make sure that the differences in course condition between drivers is as small as

At National Tour and Divisional events, drivers sharing a car are required to use a certain numbering protocol. The second driver's car number is 100 plus the first driver's number. This means that 1s are always being added and removed from the side of the car. (Photo Courtesy Bryan Heitkotter)

Course workers are required to keep a written log of on-course happenings at National Tour and Divisional events. This log is the official record of what cone penalties are to be applied to the runs. The record includes identifying which cone was hit. Here, an event official collects the form from the course workers so that a results audit can be performed. (Photo Courtesy Bryan Heitkotter)

possible. Cars are run in order of car number, from lowest to highest. A second driver in a car has a car number that is 100 plus the number of the first driver (70 and 170, for example.) Second drivers are run at least 5 minutes after the first driver returns to the grid to ensure minimal competitive advantage or disadvantage of co-driving.

Course working is different in the sense that there is a written record of the events that happen on course. Every car is recorded as it passes through a work station. If a penalty is incurred, it is recorded (including the location of the penalty) on paper as well as called in on the course radio. In timing and scoring, the radio report is checked against the paper logs to ensure accuracy of the penalties. The paper course logs are posted for drivers to check between runs. If there is a discrepancy between the posted results and the posted paper course logs, drivers can protest the results. The paper course logs are considered to be the definitive record of what happened out on course.

Impound is a procedure that gives competitors an opportunity to check for legality of their competitors' cars. After the final run of competition is complete for a class, all competitors are held in impound until final results are posted (usually around 30 minutes). In impound, competitors are required to open the hood and trunk of their car and remain in impound with their class.

During this time, competitors can visually inspect all of the cars in their class for compliance with the rules. In the event of the need to file a protest, there is a formal procedure. A protest fee must accompany the protest and a bond must be paid for any costs anticipated to verify legality of the protest. If the protest is upheld, the protest fee and bond are returned.

Impound is a procedure that is used for National Tour and Divisional events. At most events, the procedure involves opening the hood and trunk of the car and wait for results. Opening the car allows competitors to inspect the other cars in the class for legality. Here, the procedure also included removing tires from one side of the car. (Photo Courtesy Bryan Heitkotter)

Participating in many National Solo events requires a serious commitment to the sport. Friends made during these events are worth the effort. The C Prepared class, for example, is its own fraternity at National events. (Photo Courtesy Bryan Heitkotter)

ProSolo events have their runs start with a drag strip launch. The driver's reaction time counts toward the total run time. Here, a Subaru is staging. All-wheel-drive cars enjoy a significant advantage over their competition right at the starting line. (Photo Courtesy Bryan Heitkotter)

National Tour events are few and far between. The SCCA typically organizes six to eight National Tour events each season. These events are considered to be second only to the Solo National Championships in terms of prestigious events in the traditional Solo format. Much of this feel comes from the contingency prizes that are available at these events. Contingency prizes are provided by event sponsors and are awarded to qualifying participants

according to the requirements of the event sponsor. Typical sponsors are car and tire manufacturers. These companies put up modest prizes for drivers using their products who win (or finish well) at the event. These programs are administered by the SCCA and program requirements are posted online.

Overall, the reason to participate in the Divisional or National Tour events is the opportunity to compete against drivers from other regions.

Don't be intimidated by the procedural differences. Don't be concerned about the possibility of being beaten by top drivers. Growth as a driver is dependent upon taking chances and learning from the results. Divisional and National Tour events are great learning experiences.

SCCA ProSolo National Series

The SCCA ProSolo National Series is a different animal and some consider it the pinnacle of Solo in the United States. For the serious autocrosser, these events are interesting. For the dedicated drivers competing in the series, this is serious business. As the Pro name implies, there is money to be won at these events—both in contingency prizes and general prize money. These events are intended to maximize the enjoyment of the sport, but the different format and level of intensity can be overwhelming to an unprepared driver.

ProSolo pits drivers against each other in head-to-head competition. The typical event has two mirror-image courses—a left course and a right course. The event is divided into four heats. The first three heats are class competition with drivers competing against other drivers in their class. In the last heat, held on Sunday afternoon, the top drivers from each class are seeded based on class results and paired up for a bracket-racing style of eliminations.

Each of the first three heats consists of four runs for each driver. Two runs are made on each course in an alternating sequence. If a driver starts on the left course, the sequence is left, right, right, left. The order of running during the first heat is determined by car number. During the second and third heats, the

ProSolo events feature side-by-side action. Drivers compete on parallel courses. A driver's best run from each course determines his or her total time. In this case, two ladies are competing in the indexed L2 class. Their times will be compared using the ProSolo index, which is similar to but slightly different than the PAX/RTP Index. (Photo Courtesy Bryan Heitkotter)

Successful competitors at a ProSolo event will find their car ends up in an extended impound process. The cars that qualify for eliminations are impounded after class competition is complete but before the elimination rounds start. In impound, adjustments are severely limited. Adding fuel is one of the few legal things competitors can do to their car. (Photo Courtesy Bryan Heitkotter)

Sunday afternoon brings elimination rounds, called the Super Challenge and Ladies Challenge. The top 32 open-class drivers (seeded based on largest margin of victory down to largest margin of defeat) are placed into a single elimination bracket and head-to-head competition determines the Super Challenge winner. The Ladies Challenge is seeded with the top drivers from the Ladies Classes and is run in a similar manner. Prize money is awarded to top qualifiers and top finishers in these challenge brackets.

The actual elimination rounds are run like bracket racing with slower cars being given a head start. Each driver is given a dial in based on the fastest raw times in their class. A fast run with a downed cone doesn't help you out in class competition, but it does count when determining a class' dial in. With the pairs set, the dial ins are input into the starting system. Barring penalties, the first driver back to the finish line wins the pair. After the first run, the two drivers swap sides to eliminate any advantage of one course over the other. A red light—starting

sequence of running is based on class position with first and second paired up together. The first two heats are held on Saturday with the third heat taking place on Sunday morning.

In the ProSolo format, drivers launch into the course from a standing start. Drivers stage in the same manner as drag racers. When the start sequence is initiated, three amber lights are illuminated followed by the green light. Run times are measured from the time the green light is illuminated, so a good start is crucial. Also, with the start of the course being generally straight for around 200 feet, a solid launch from the starting line can be crucial.

Another quirk of this format is that the fastest time from each course is counted, regardless of when that time was recorded. A driver who has a poor Saturday can redeem himself with good runs on Sunday morning and win the event. Also, with six runs on each course, most drivers are very aggressive. It only takes one run on each side and most drivers can get

a clean run with six chances at it, even being very aggressive. The SCCA has begun implementing variations on this format. Variations that have been seen so far include a single course format with the best run from each session being counted. In this case, a driver has to be good in every session to win.

At ProSolo events, cars with minimum weights are checked for rules compliance. Each car must be legal after each of the three sessions. The penalty for being under weight is typically having the times from that session disallowed. (Photo Courtesy Bryan Heitkotter)

Two G Stock competitors launch themselves from the starting line. The side-by-side competition of ProSolo makes it more interesting for the spectators. This is the only type of autocross event where the audience can actually see who is ahead while the runs are happening. (Photo Courtesy Bryan Heitkotter)

The Solo National Championships are a big event. Competitors work to be fully focused before leaving the grid. With large classes and close competition, a driver needs every advantage he or she can get. (Photo Courtesy Bryan Heitkotter)

before the green light illuminates—results in automatic disqualification. The penalty for a cone has varied from two seconds per cone to automatic disqualification. Breaking out, running a time faster than the dial-in time, is permitted a certain number of times. Exceeding the allowed number of break outs results in disqualification.

The ProSolo National Series culminates in a finale held in conjunction with the Solo National Championships. The top drivers from each class, based on points accrued during the season, battle for a year-end prize fund. The top points earners in each class are crowned champions. Additionally, the top points earners in the challenges are awarded a separate overall championship. Being a ProSolo champion means performing well during at least three events and no ProSolo champion can be crowned on luck alone.

SCCA Solo National Championships

For those who aren't fully enamored with the ProSolo series, the SCCA Solo National Championships are the crown jewel of the sport. The event typically draws more than 1,000 entries. It's scheduled in mid to late September and lasts a week. For an individual competitor, the event is run in much the same manner as a Divisional or National Tour event. In fact, Divisional and National Tour events are formatted as they are so that competitors know what to expect at the Solo National Championships. Solo Nationals, however, is so large that the competitors need to be divided into two groups—those who compete early in the week and those who compete at the end of the week.

For more than a decade, the SCCA Solo National Championships have been held in Kansas. First, the event was held in Salina and then it moved to Topeka. With both the SCCA National office and the SCCA Club Racing National Championships, The

The SCCA Solo National Championships are a significant commitment in terms of time and money, especially for people living on the coasts. These autocross cars were loaded on a transporter to make their way to Topeka, Kansas. While this was expensive, it saved the car owners two days of travel each way. (Photo Courtesy Bryan Heitkotter)

The Solo National Championships are so large that two courses are run simultaneously. The Mini in the foreground is running on the West course while the BMW in the background runs on the East course. Participants drive one course each day and times are combined to determine the final results.

With so many competitors attending the Solo Nationals, congestion is inevitable. This includes the course walks. The event runs over five days (one for course walking only and four of competition). The mid-day course walking breaks are typically packed with competitors trying to get in one more walk before they compete. (Photo Courtesy Bryan Heitkotter)

Runoffs, located in Topeka, it is unlikely that the Solo Nationals will move any time soon. Because of this location, most competitors have significant travel distances to reach the event, but at least no one has to travel the length of the country to attend.

With the format of the event being similar to Divisional and National Tour events, the competitors are left to deal with the size of

the event. The festivities traditionally start on a Saturday and end on a Friday. Saturday and Sunday have commonly had warm up events where drivers can practice on the Solo Nationals surface. The courses are built on Sunday afternoon and

are open for walking on Monday morning. Meanwhile, Registration and Technical Inspection are under way, with emphasis on those competitors who will compete during the first half of the week. Tuesday is the beginning of competition. Both courses run simultaneously with roughly one quarter of the drivers competing on each course. On Wednesday, the competitors switch courses to complete their competition. Wednesday night brings an awards banquet to honor the national champions. On Thursday, the routine starts over with "day 1" action on both courses. Friday is just like Wednesday except that the paddock is empty by the time the awards banquet starts.

Aside from the schedule, competitors need to adapt to the size of the event. With over 1,000 drivers in attendance, it's easy to become overwhelmed. It's not uncommon to see classes with more than 40 entries. The depth of talent is also intimidating.

Competition is intense and fields are deep. It is common for a popular class to have more than 40 entries at the Solo Nationals. Often a class will have several National Champions vying to be recrowned. In this case, both drivers of the car are National Champions. (Photo Courtesy Bryan Heitkotter)

A driver enjoys a moment of rest before launching into the course. The Solo National Championships can be stomach turning or pleasant, depending on your expectations. It is tough to be disappointed when the intent is to have fun.

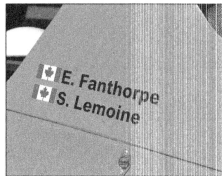

Canadian participation in autocross events is pretty common. With limited access to events in Canada, Canadian competitors are often seen attending events south of the border. These F Modified competitors show national pride by displaying a small Canadian flag on the car. Canadian competitors have been relatively successful with several SCCA National Championship trophies traveling across the border.

Most classes are stacked with season veterans and often have more than one National Champion.

So, to make the most of the National Championships, show up early and get the feel of the event. Find a friend from home and have him or her show you around. Have fun with it! You'll meet people from regions all around the United States and Canada. It's worthwhile as a chance to meet friends regardless of how you finish. Have low expectations and relax. Remember, it's rare for a first-timer to win a Championship, so some of the pressure is off!

North of the Border

Canada isn't exactly a hotbed for autocross. That doesn't mean, however, that there isn't any autocross north of the border. With around two dozen active clubs and a large area to cover, Canadian autocrossers can expect to travel a bit to attend events. While the clubs are widely scattered, the competitors are dedicated.

The leading sanctioning body in Canada is ASN Canada FIA. ASN Canada calls autocross the Autoslalom portion of their Solosport program. There are five affiliate clubs of ASN Canada that participate in Solosport. These clubs are scattered from the Maritime Provinces all the way to British Columbia. With the exception of classing rules, the ASN Canada Autoslalom rules are very similar to the SCCA Solo Rules. ASN Canada has a completely different set of car preparation rules from the SCCA, but the overall concept is the same. Cars are distinguished by type of car and preparation with the intent of providing close competition.

Information regarding ASN Canada and their affiliate clubs can be found on the ASN Canada website: www.ASNCanada.com.

Autocross is a hobby. It should be fun. There is lots of talk about rules and work assignments, but you should try to make it fun. Little things like having a themed event can really lighten the atmosphere and make the event feel like a gathering rather than a competition. (Photo Courtesy Bryan Heitkotter)

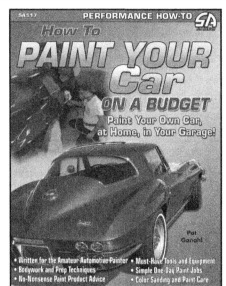

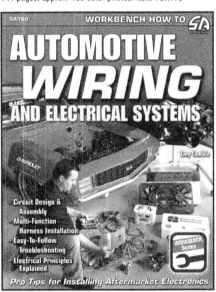

CPSIA information can be obtained
at www.ICGtesting.com
Printed in the USA
BVOW09s1101060717

488538BV00007B/71/P